CIRCUS DAYS
&
CHIMP ANTICS

By
DAVID HIBLING

Line one publishing ltd.

ISBN 0 907036 31 7

Published by
Line One Publishing Ltd,
Unit 2, Mead Park,
Mead Road,
Cheltenham,
Glos. GL53 7EF

CIRCUS DAYS
&
CHIMP ANTICS

By
DAVID HIBLING

Line one
publishing ltd.

ISBN 0 907036 31 7

Published by
Line One Publishing Ltd,
Unit 2, Mead Park,
Mead Road,
Cheltenham,
Glos. GL53 7EF

CONTENTS

ACKNOWLEDGEMENTS

There are many people to whom thanks are owed for assistance given to me whilst writing 'Circus Days and Chimp Antics'. I would like to mention one or two by name; Malcolm Cook and all at Line One for a great deal of encouragement, Roger and Mary Cawley for 'checking facts', Jack Denyer for a never-ending supply of typing paper, typewriter ribbons and correction fluid! Peter Denyer for patience and understanding. This book is dedicated to my parents Janis and Barry.

David Hibling 1986

Taking a break.
(Mike Foster)

FOREWORD

I read the manuscript of this book in one session that took me well into the night. I just could not stop reading and the reason is a simple one. This is the story of a man who really did what we would all have loved to do: he joined the circus. He became part of a magical world that most of us only visit and then dream about. But here is not just the story of the glamour that we see, it is much more the story of hard work and patience.

The patience comes in the training and handling of animals. The truth is written simply and in such a way that you can feel the love of this trainer for animals that are more than pets and more like family or friends. I worked with Fred and Betsy, chimpanzees now enjoying retirement and living in luxury like two old theatre pros, which is of course what they are. I loved them and the way they worked me into their act and made me look so stupid! Animal lovers take note: they had a far better contract with the BBC than I did — they had it written in that they had to go to bed in the afternoon whilst the mere humans had to keep on working.

People who work for Animal Rights Societies should be made to read this book. It's an honest account of circus and 'zoo' life and shows the care and attention that most animals receive. The honesty shows in the writing. There will be some cruelty in some circus somewhere because, sadly, no section of society is perfect, but mostly, thank goodness, the treatment is as described in these pages. There are far more cruel happenings in the world of family pets and the 'bad guys' in the circus are rapidly weeded out.

I am honoured to have been asked to write this foreword and now you can sit back, relax, and join the circus.

Paul Daniels

Best Wishes Paul Daniels

Chapter 1

A Letter from Chipperfields

It was a typical, clear, crisp Swiss autumn morning in 1978. I was eating a breakfast of croissants and coffee, half listening to Mandy who was worried about the health of Poco one of the dolphins in her care, and half listening for the sound of the motorbike on which an intrepid, if ageing, plump village postman delivered the mail.

Mandy and I had spent almost a year working with dolphins and sealions in the unique Swiss aqua-circus called "Flippershow". A travelling concern it had replaced a sawdust ring with an enormous circular tank in which a pair of dolphins performed. There was a stage, on which acts, amongst them a trio of sealions with which I worked, went through their paces. The show was now in Winterquarters at Lipperswil, a tiny hamlet near the Swiss/German border and set against a backdrop of spectacular mountain scenery. Apart from the circus buildings the hamlet consisted of just a few houses, one or two gasthouses, a sawmill, church, pig farm and post office. It was all very tranquil, but Mandy and I were restless.

We had had one or two disagreements with the management and had now decided to return home to England. With a little bit of luck our postman would be bringing some much awaited news regarding possible work.

I had recently read in a newspaper sent from home, that the world famous showman Jimmy Chipperfield was to present a brand new circus to tour England in 1979. This would star his daughters, Mary an animal trainer with the highest reputation, and her younger sister Margaret, who was following the family tradition of training animals. I had worked for Mary a few years earlier as an apprentice trainer/groom and had written to her after reading the newspaper article, to see if there was any opportunity of working in her father's new show.

I helped Mandy clear away the breakfast things and stepped out of the caravan which we shared, and cast a glance down the lane to see if I could spy the postman. Shortly, I heard the familiar 'phut phut phut' of the little motorcycle and around the corner came the man himself. I welcomed him with a quick "Greuzi", the Swiss friendly greeting which does not seem to translate into the English language. He handed me our mail before carrying on to disperse the contents of his sack amongst the other caravans. Sure enough there was a letter from the Chipperfields. It was from one of the firm's directors, Roger Cawley, Mary Chipperfield's husband, and it offered me the chance of training a group of chimpanzees.

Adolf, Dedi and Taxi, the Flipper Show sealions. (Author's collection)

I was at once excited and apprehensive. I was more used to sealions and dolphins, but chimpanzees were a different 'kettle of fish' entirely. Not for the first time in my life I had to make a major decision, and quickly. I telephoned Roger, accepted his offer, managed to obtain a job for Mandy with the circus horses and in a couple of weeks we were on an aeroplane heading for Gatwick airport.

My breakfast partner of that morning was Mandy Moore, a friend and colleague of longstanding. Previously we had worked at the Brighton Aquarium on what had been our first jobs since leaving school. In my eyes the Aquarium was the first step on a road that would, hopefully, lead to 'stardom' in the circus ring.

As a child I always had a passion for anything connected with entertainment and an equally overwhelming love for animals, which combined to make me an avid fan of the circus. Apart from an uncle who worked producing television and theatre productions I had no family connection with entertainment, but from an early age I was determined that in one form or another, I would have a job in a circus. To me the circus was *the* most exciting form of show business, and as animals were vital to the world of sawdust, I was well and truly hooked; more than that I was obsessed. I ate, drank, and slept 'circuses'. I would stage circus performances in my back garden. The Hibling Circus, patronised by patient family and neighbours, would feature my schoolfriends as acrobats and clowns, my faithful pet dog Brandy would stand in for the elephants, lions and tigers with an expert display of hoop and hurdle jumping.

I collected circus posters and programmes, my school essays somehow always managed to include a circus in them and my parents were pestered into taking me to any circus that came within a 50 mile radius of my childhood home in Newhaven, Sussex. My mother Janis, could have become one of Britain's premier circus critics in the late sixties. She had seen so many shows; Billy Smart's, Chipperfield's, Sir Robert Fossett's, Weight's, Hoffman's and Roberts Brothers — we saw them all. Although I believe my father initially hoped this all consuming passion was a passing phase I would grow out of, both my parents gave me great support in my ambitions and have shared my circus experiences happily. I keep an everlasting memory of my mother, clad in raincoat and Wellington boots, struggling to lead a very mischievous camel from the stables to the circus ring, lead in one hand, handbag firmly held in the other.

However as a youngster my biggest influence, as far as the circus was concerned, was a retired circus man, Captain England. 'Skipper' as he was known to everyone was a real life schoolboy's hero. He had once been the Master of the last British cargo ship using sails. The vessel itself sank off the coast of Plymouth, causing the tragic loss of one of his daughters. The other, Inge-lise, being saved and later to find fame as one of the world's most respected circus solo trapeze artistes. After the shipwreck 'Skipper' became General Manager of several British circuses amongst them Billy Smart's, the show, which in my youth, epitomised 'circus'. By the time I knew him he had retired from the circus and, together with his adoring wife 'Bill', (a nickname from sailing days) had set up home in Newhaven where he had a sailing loft where he made much sought after sails for yachts. Almost every Sunday afternoon as a child I would visit them in their snug little caravan on the cliffs at Newhaven, within earshot of his beloved sea. I would spend hours listening to seafaring tales and circus stories. After tea, my head spinning with all the romance of the sawdust ring, I would return home and feel even more determined to join the circus.

Shortly before he died, he and Bill moved to a village near Swindon, and it was a great thrill for me to be able to perform in front of them with the chimp act when the circus paid a visit to the town. In true chimp fashion they decided to misbehave, they squabbled in the ring, pretended to be deaf when I gave them cues and Anna did one of her impromptu stripteases! (More of which later.)

All the same, I knew that 'Skipper' was proud of the little boy who had once shadowed him so closely, now grown up and had joined the circus. When he died, I realised just how much he had given me, how as a child he was so kind and patient with me. A larger than life character, I have fond memories of him, and treasure the gift of a model circus with which he surprised me one Christmas. This is a beautifully made Big Top with all the trimmings that he lovingly created for me.

The circus life was still a way off however as I finished school exams and made by way into the big wide world. I had applied for a job as assistant keeper to aquatic mammals at the Brighton Dolphinarium/Aquarium, not far from my Newhaven home, and in due course found myself working with dolphins, seals, sealions and penguins. I must admit that the original intention was to use the Dolphinarium as a temporary stopgap before finding employment in a circus, but I soon fell under the dolphins' spell, fascinated by the almost ghost-like way their sleek streamlined bodies swam through the water. That, combined with the clown-like impudence of ten Californian sealions was more than enough to entrap a 16 year old school leaver.

At that time the Dolphinarium/Aquarium was staffed by three young and attractive women, Mandy my future Swiss companion, Elaine Atcheler, and the inimitable Jackie Goulder. All three became and remain loyal friends, with Jackie, in her position as Head Keeper at the Aquarium, playing a great part in shaping my outlook on working with animals, becoming my mentor and teacher.

I am indebted to her guidance and instruction. Jackie was a former S.E.N., but soon had to confess that her true affection was with animals, and if she was not careful she would become more concerned with a sick pet at home, than with the ailments of the patients on her ward. So, she decided that a career with animals was where her future lay. Her particular passion was with all forrns of water life and spent several years apprenticed to some of the most experienced aquarists, before accepting the position at Brighton. There she was responsible for the daily care of all the animals in the exhibition. I firmly believe that at that particular time in the Aquarium's long history the standard of animal husbandry was at an all-time high due to the dedication of Jackie to her work. I am sure she would forgive me if I described her as a slight eccentric in the true animal keeper style. A beautiful woman, at work she cared little for personal appearance, gold rimmed glasses tied up with string and hair held back firmly with elastic bands. She was happiest wearing old clothes with her elbows plunged into some fish tank rearranging the floral decor, chatting merrily to the tank's inhabitants, all of whom I swear she knew individually.

Jackie was tireless in her approach to work which was a good training for me, preparing me for the exhausting schedules I would later encounter with Mary Chipperfield. Jackie was also very patient with the young man who followed her around like a puppy, eager to learn from her wide experience of animal keeping. She taught me a vital lesson. That is, no matter how long one works with animals you will never stop learning, and it was Jackie who encouraged me to consume all the knowledge I could with the help of books. She herself was a dedicated bookworm and it was not uncommon for her to have three or four books on the go at one time.

Jackie realised that intelligent, captive animals needed stimulation and she was responsible for the training of the ten sealions, and to an extent the dolphins. She did not have much prior knowledge of training, most of her skills being self taught but she possessed all the qualifications of an animal trainer; patience, a great understanding of animals and a deep rooted love for them. She was happy to pass on her knowledge of training, and I learned so much from observing her at work, sharing her joy when an animal mastered a trick. Occasions such as when Honey the sealion first mastered the art of ball balancing, or when Baby the dolphin, first pulled a little boat across the pool were moments of celebration long remembered.

My days at the Aquarium hold many fond memories with much fun and laughter. The three women enriched my working life and helped to create an atmosphere in which learning was easy, and helped me to build a strong foundation on which my career with animals would grow.

Like myself, Mandy was a local, Sussex born and bred. She had filled her house with pets as a child, and today is still only happy when surrounded by animals. Mandy, petite, dark haired and eyed, was very attractive, and I am sure many a young man watching the daily performances given by the dolphins, which she co-presented, kept one eye on her as they were put through their paces.

My third colleague, Elaine, I often felt was far more complex than either Jackie or Mandy. To me, Mandy always seemed chirpy, bright, content with all aspects of her life. Jackie was very intelligent, secure in her work and private life and dealt rationally with any problems that occurred in either. Elaine on the other hand, was at that time insecure, capable of great highs and lows. In many ways I was able to identify with her and we became very close friends. Her love of animals was as deep as anyone else's yet I think that deep inside she had nagging doubts about her role in animal husbandry, feeling that she ought to be doing more to help wild animals. Elaine, like all of us, was appalled at the horror and butchery connected with commercial whaling. It was largely due to her efforts that a petition was organised at the Dolphinarium, signed by thousands of visitors, and sent to the Ministry of Agriculture and Fisheries expressing horror at the slaughter of wild dolphins and whales and calling for an end to whaling in general.

Elaine is now living in Australia where she is actively involved in various preservation groups. I miss her. We shared the same sense of humour and I recall many happy days spent in her company.

There were of course other staff employed in secretarial, maintainance, and managerial positions at the Dolphinarium, and from time to time the animal staff was augmented by others, yet none of these made any lasting impression on me, unlike my three workmates.

We worked hard and the days were long. There was what seemed like a ton of fish, food for the dolphins and other marine mammals that had to be sorted and gutted each morning. The pools in which the Harbour seals and penguins lived had to be scrubbed clean and then refilled with gallons of fresh (but filtered) seawater, pumped in from the ocean which was a hundred yards away from the building. Late at night, before we left for home, the filters on the larger dolphin and sealion pools had to be checked and 'backwashed', the cleaning process which ensured the filters could carry out their duties efficiently. In between we put the dolphins and sealions through their paces for the public at regular intervals and we took turns in caring for literally thousands of tropical, freshwater and marine fish that inhabited the Aquarium section.

The Aquarium part of the complex was built in Victorian times and consisted of large tanks for fish and reptiles, pools for sealions, seals and penguins. Dolphins were first exhibited in the pool now used by sealions, but in 1968 a large luxuriant dolphin pool was built at one end of the building in what had formerly been a motor museum. The large pool could be viewed on two levels, there being an arena seating approximately a thousand people, and below, large windows built into the side of the pool enabled the public to watch the dolphins swim and play underwater.

The dolphin shows given through the day lasted about 30 minutes and consisted of the animals displaying their leaping and jumping abilities, as well as retrieving objects from the water, ball games and even singing.

It was these shows that gave me my first taste of entertaining the public and also my first opportunities of speaking to an audience as the trainers would give a running commentary throughout the dolphin display.

I enjoyed the shows immensely and working with the dolphins was a unique experience. Each day we swam with them and at the Dolphinarium I learned to scuba-dive which was exhilerating, and to be able to swim with the animals underwater at leisure was something almost indescribably beautiful.

For their part the animals enjoyed the company of the human swimmers and would play 'tag' with us and allow us to hitch a ride on their backs.

Unlike the girls, I was not actively involved in the actual training of the dolphins, but I was able to train the two Harbour seals Sunshine and Yogi to do a few simple tricks. The seals, without the agility of their cousins the sealions, could only master simple feats such as retrieving rings thrown into the water, spinning and diving on cue, while Sunshine mastered the art of blowing a horn! Harbour seals, native to British shores are very appealing animals with huge puppy-like eyes. Smaller than the other British seal, the Grey seal, they have large domed head and short muzzle.

Like all animals the training of the seals was a question of patience, gentle coaxing and reward. In Sunshine and Yogi's case the reward was chunks of herring or mackerel taken from their daily ration. Both animals were very affectionate in a dog-like sort of fashion.

It was whilst working at the Aquarium, that I experienced love for the first time. Sadly any relationship that might have developed between myself and the young lady who fell head-over-heels in love with me was beset by problems. There was a language barrier for a start. Whilst I would whisper sweet nothings into Lily's ear she would answer me in a tone that resembled a soft braying noise. Lily was a South African Jackass penguin. Actually, in all honesty it was not *me* that Lily first fell in love with, it was my Wellington boot! There was an uneven number of male/female penguins kept at the Aquarium and sadly Lily had no mate. It never really seemed to worry her until she struck up the relationship with my boot, and each morning as I cleaned out the penguin pool she would dash after me and nibble

Yogi and Sunshine harbour seals.
(Author's collection)

lovingly at the black shiny Wellington. Whether or not she could see a reflection of herself in the plastic, I do not know, but she was enamoured. In time her attentions would spread to the occupant of the boot and she would utter the distinctive bray that gave the Jackass penguin its name whenever I entered the pool. In quiet moments we would sit and chat about all sorts of things, but I won't go into details — far be it from me to divulge a lady's secrets.

Happily, two other penguins felt the call of love and produced an egg which was cause for great excitement. Rosie, who had laid the egg was a very attentive mother, and we all hoped, for her sake that the egg was fertile. We counted off the days during incubation and to everyone's delight the egg hatched and a smelly little chick emerged. No Easter chick this one, he was very greasy and smelt strongly of fish! However Rosie and all of us thought he was beautiful.

Rosie was an excellent mother and raised him herself, doting on the little bird. A local newspaper ran a competition to find a name and he was aptly called Pongo.

Another chick that soon became resident in the Aquarium was Squiggles a Herring gull that Jackie hand-reared. Squiggles was a real character, with a distinct personality of his own. For some reason he failed to produce the natural oily substance which gulls have to keep their feathers waterproof, so consequently he sank everytime he tried to swim in water for more than a few minutes, as his feathers became well and truly waterlogged. Jackie, his surrogate mother was besotted by him and he eventually moved into her flat, which prompted the staff to write a little ditty about one of Squiggles' more unpleasant habits,

"All around my flat
there is evidence of a seagull,
and all around my flat,
you can see where he has been . . ."

Jackie's affection for the bird was only matched by his affection for her. He would emit an ear-piercing scream each time he saw her, and at night would sleep tucked up against her head. Each morning he would travel to work on the bus with Jackie, riding in a converted cat basket. In fact he accompanied Jackie all over the place, even once as far as London to sit through a performance of the Circus World Championships, the circus olympics held each autumn.

During the daytime, Squiggles had the run of the behind-the-scenes of the Aquarium. He usually joined the staff for teabreak, having his own mug of sweet tea in which he would swirl his beak. Tragically, whilst enjoying a holiday with friends of Jackie at the Dolphinarium on Clacton pier, he was killed when a storm caused part of the pier to collapse.

Jackie kept a variety of pets, such as a strikingly handsome Royal python, to a one-legged jackdaw whom she had rescued, but none of her pets caused as much trouble as did her collection of mice.

Jackie decided one day that it would be fun to breed mice. She started her hobby at home, but such was her success that the population of rodents grew and grew and soon became too large for her tiny flat. She moved it into the Aquarium, where unknown to the Management, she stored it in one of the many large disused rooms that are found in abundance behind the rows of fish tanks in the old Victorian building, and which were seldom visited by anyone.

All went well, and Jackie soon began to breed a variety of strikingly coloured mice. Then, one afternoon, a mouse with an inbred Houdini streak, broke out of his cage and began to explore, his travels leading him to one of the two admission kiosks much to the alarm of the elderly cashier, a lady of nervous disposition at the best of times. Pandamonium broke out. A search party led by senior members of management followed, intent on covering the entire building until the culprit was caught. Jackie, horrified that the safari would discover not only one, but indeed several hundred mice hidden away behind the row of 'Native Saltwater' tanks, called Mandy and I up on the internal telephone system and begged assistance. With all the speed of the seventh cavalry we rushed to her aid.

The intrepid band of mouse-catchers was getting perilously close to the source of the first mouse's appearance. Jackie went to "assist" in the search doing her best to guide the party away from the mice menagerie whilst Mandy and I attempted to remove the cages. Jackie often resorted to emitting an almost hysterical scream at the apparent sighting of a mouse sending the hunters scampering off in the wrong direction. Meanwhile, with cages tucked under our arms Mandy and I gave several families of mice a free conducted tour of the building lasting a couple of hours and keeping slightly ahead of our pursuers!

The search party eventually gave up the chase, and not long after Jackie sold the collection to a local pet shop. Interestingly enough the original escapee was never caught, and for all I know he could still be resident somewhere behind the fish tanks.

In time, I felt a need to expand my knowledge of animals, and thought I should find work with other species of animals, and applied for a job that was advertised by Drusillas Zoopark, looking after varied animals in the Sussex zoological collection.

Drusillas is a delightful place, not far from the 'chocolate-box' village of Alfriston. It opened originally as a tea garden expanding over the years until today it is a compact pleasure park with a small zoo, adventure playground, narrow gauge railway, craft centre, bakery, pottery, garden centre and restaurant where their famous cream teas are still available. The park buildings are lovingly cared for, most of them having thatched roofs and flowers are in abundance everywhere.

The zoo has a surprisingly large variety of animals in the collection, monkeys, racoons, coati-mundis, llamas, lemurs, wallabies and hundreds of birds, including penguins and flamingoes. There is a nocturnal house, and an exhibit that displays rare breeds of British farm animals including cattle, pigs, sheep and goats.

I spent a year at the park, quite happy to bury myself in the countryside looking after all the animals with particular responsibility for the monkeys.

The following winter however, two of the dolphins in the Brighton collection, Prinny and Missus surprised everyone by giving a baby to the pool. I was asked to return to give the staff a hand as all was not well with the new arrival. The new-born dolphin was not suckling properly and it was discovered that for some reason Missus' milk had dried up. After consultation with vets it was decided that the baby would have to be hand-reared — if possible. A Dutch dolphinarium had been successful in rearing baby dolphins and a substitute milk formula was dispatched to Brighton. The little animal was moved to a shallow pool within sight of Missus, where staff would be able to attempt to bottle feed him. A round-the-clock vigil was kept with staff spending 24 hours a day at the building for the next few weeks, snatching meals and sleep whenever and wherever possible.

At first the baby took to bottle feeding with no problems. It was discovered that the easiest way to suckle the baby was to lie flat in the water with the animal supported on our chests.

Sadly, the animal began to weaken and after a while it refused the milk offered and eventually the little dolphin died. At the time, a dolphin birth in English dolphinariums was a rare occurrence. Since then several establishments, notably Windsor Safari Park have had dolphins born and reared successfully. This knowledge was unavailable to us at the time, and even if it had been it would have been of small comfort. An air of gloom hung over us all, and the depression was as great in the pool as out.

The death of the animal hit the girls hard, maternal instincts had been aroused by the feeding of the little animal, and after days and nights of tending him, to watch him give up the struggle to live was heartbreaking.

I stayed at the Dolphinarium for a few months after the death, but I felt very restless inside. I had received as a Christmas present a copy of Jimmy Chipperfield's autobiography 'My Wild Life', and one evening in the late spring I wrote a letter to him to see if he could offer me work.

I was offered a job at the Longleat Safari Park, a position I accepted and for the second and last time I said goodbye to the Aquarium. Longleat was Britain's first safari park, opened in the early sixties, a joint venture between Lord Bath and Jimmy Chipperfield, whose brainchild the revolutionary concept of safari parks had been. Jimmy Chipperfield had felt the public would respond to the idea of them being caged in cars, driving through large reserves of free-roaming lions, tigers, giraffe, elephants etc. At the time all the so-called experts thought him quite mad, and that the idea would never take off.

Well, take off it did and millions of people have now seen the 'Lions of Longleat' and safari parks, many of them designed and operated by Chipperfields have sprung up all over the world. It would not be an understatement to say that the parks had revolutionised zoological thinking, with many of Britain's zoos building enclosures nowadays which follow safari park lines. Longleat and the other British parks have spectacular breeding successes with lions, giraffe antelope and even rhino. I find it very amusing that a circus showman should have been responsible for such a development in zoological husbandry, and not for the first time this century had a circus man, rather than a zoologist, made a major contribution to animal keeping. Fifty years earlier, former circus man, Hagenbeck pioneered the removal of cages and their replacement with open ditches in his zoo in Hamburg, Germany.

Arriving at Longleat I was determined to make a good impression, and told everyone of my intention. My first day at the park I was asked if I could drive a tractor. Not wishing to appear useless I replied "Yes". I could drive, but had only ever driven a small tractor once before, and then only for about five minutes. I soon found myself in the driver's seat of a very large tractor. Nervously, but determined, I set off for the rhino reserve where I was to keep an eye on the herd,

Rhino's at Longleat Safari Park.
(David Jamieson)

following them with the tractor making sure they did not interfere with the public and vice-versa. I chugged along behind the rhinos, and by mid-morning the sun shining, my confidence was soaring — tractor driving? Nothing to it!

After lunch the rhino herd decided to descend the slope at the far end of the reserve, and keeper Hibling naturally followed on behind. For some reason, as I told them in the ambulance afterwards, I failed to locate the brakes. Down the hill I sped, faster and faster scattering the indignant rhino ahead of me. I did eventually stop; crashing through the iron gate which obviously helped slow me down, but it was the passing lorry that finally brought the runaway tractor to a halt. I was lucky as I suffered only minor bruising and shock, and was in hospital just for the one night. The story of Hibling and the tractor is still remembered in the safari park, especially as on the way out of the park that afternoon my final words to Mike Foster, then head keeper at Longleat, was,

"I only wanted to make a good impression!"

Shortly after the tractor incident I was dispatched to Mary Chipperfield's circus winter quarters and training farm in the little village of Over Wallop in Hampshire. I suppose they thought with Mary keeping an eye on me I was unlikely to cause too much damage! I was at last fulfilling my ambition to join a circus but, at the expense of several Chipperfield vehicles.

At that time Mary was busy training animals to star in a summer tour of a new circus, being operated by Gerry Cottle. Mr. Cottle at that time was one of Britain's leading lights in the circus and was expanding his enterprise to include a second touring unit. A deal had been struck with Mary, whereby Gerry would supply circus equipment and engage a company of trapeze artistes, trick cyclists, jugglers and clowns, and Mary would train animals for the show and star in the programme too. Mary had been very busy at the winter quarters and had groups of tigers, horses, camels, bulls, elephants, llamas, monkeys and even a giraffe in training.

Such a comprehensive collection needed a team of people to look after it and I was given the responsibility of caring for the giraffe, yak, Highland bull and the six tigers.

As a young circus fan, Mary Chipperfield had been one of my idols and I had collected photographs of her in the manner of my friends who chased after photos of football or pop stars. To actually be working for her was a bit unnerving to begin with, especially as she can be rather formidable as a boss!

She is very much the perfectionist, and very short-tempered if the humans who work for her fail to come up to scratch. She certainly kept her staff on their toes, absolutely tireless herself, she was usually the first person up in the morning and the last to leave the stables at night. On Sundays, when the pace of work slowed down a little, any

Mary Chipperfield with Bengal tiger. *(David Jamieson)*

free time she had she would be found cleaning harness in the tack room preferring to be in the company of her animals than going off somewhere to relax a little.

With her animals, she had endless patience, and as part of my duties was to assist in the training I had every opportunity to study the way she worked. Like all good animal trainers she tended to shout at her assistants if the slightest thing went wrong in training. It was nothing personal, training animals is a long process and months of hard work with an animal can be ruined if a trainer should lose his or her temper with a pupil if something has gone amiss in the training session. To relieve tempers it is far more profitable to take things out on long suffering assistants, blaming them for any mishaps rather than the animals. Good staff will always understand and I received my fair share of being shouted at. Mind you, it can be a little frustrating to be accused of setting a pedestal wrongly when an animal refuses to mount it, when one suspects the animal is merely being bloody-minded!

To Mary the comfort of the animals took precedence over the comfort of her staff, her eagle eye never missing a thing. Woe betide a groom whose animal was not sufficiently clean. She checked up on everyone, and she had an uncanny way of simply looking at an animal and telling whether or not it had been properly watered or fed. She expected total devotion to work from her staff, and standards were so

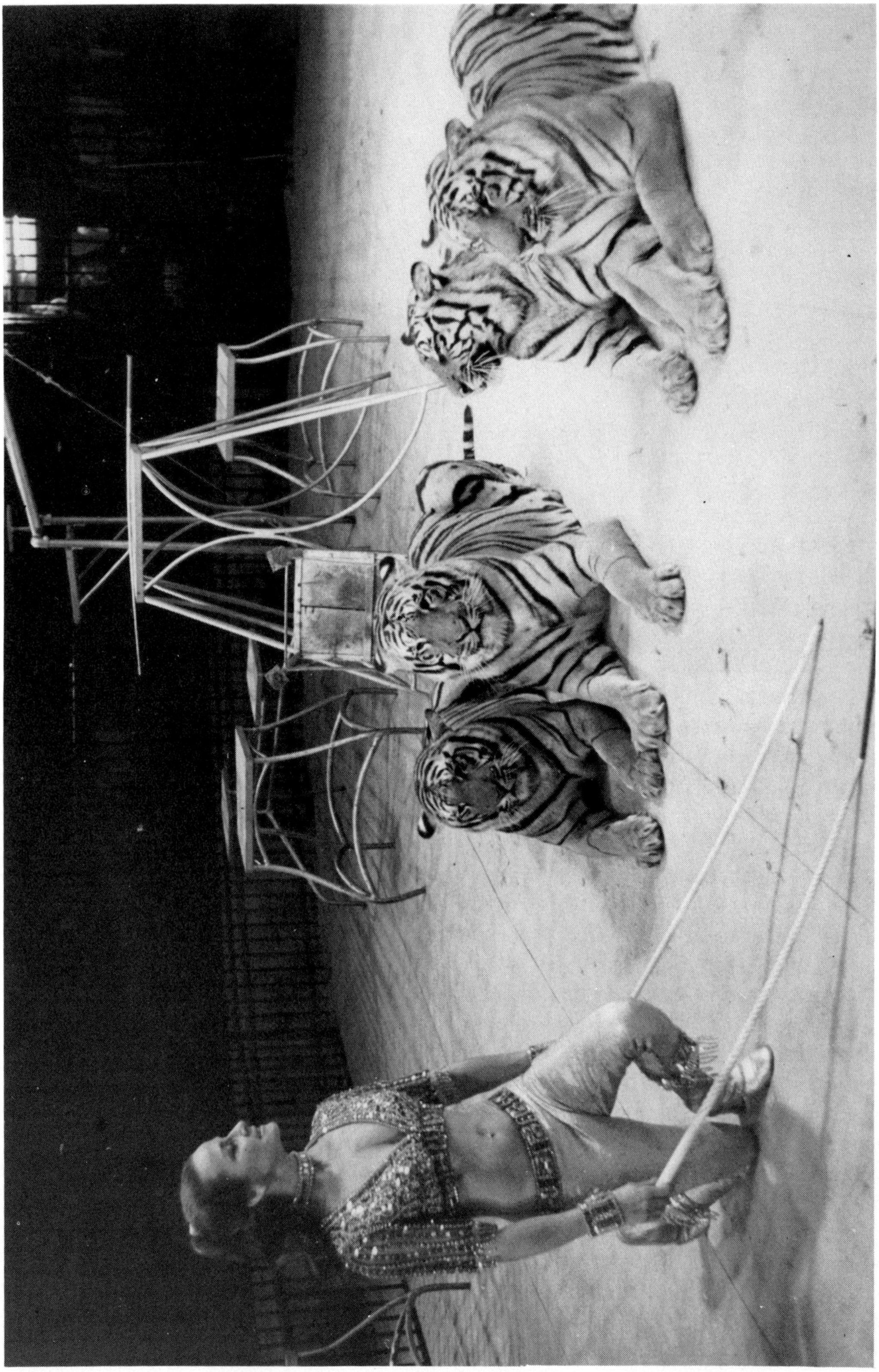

Mary Chipperfield with tigers at Blackpool Tower.

(David Jamieson)

high that many staff fell by the wayside. Those that kept up the pace included some who had worked with Mary for most of their lives and who are still on her payroll today.

Amongst these is Ron Brown, a long-term friend of Mary, herself an expert animal trainer, specially of animals supplied by Chipperfields to work in feature films. Ron, a rugged old man who always had a cigarette hanging from his lips (the only person who could dare defy Mary in this respect, she having a hatred of the habit of smoking) and who once suffered a stroke and carried on working without telling anyone. Ron is today caretaker of the Over Wallop farm and has special interest in caring for the wild animals, the lions, tigers, leopards and bears.

Mary had three girls looking after her horses on that tour. Julia Randell whose special task was grooming Mary's two high school horses, Pedro and Amber who performed in an intricate display, the circus world's equivalent of dressage. Lorraine Reeves was a young lady who would delight everyone by arriving at the stables at the crack of dawn complete with elaborate make-up, manicured nails and neatly coiffured hair, only to start mucking-out.

Lorraine had a very good sense of humour, and was one of the very few people I know who actually had the nerve to answer Mary back during a training session. Lorraine had to position the three tubs on which a trio of zebras were to stand, whilst the giraffe weaved in and out between them. On seeing that the pedestals were too close together, Mary lost her temper and shouted at Lorraine demanding how on earth the giraffe was going to get through each one. Lorraine, with her thick Hampshire accent dryly replied, "He'll 'ave to breathe in won't 'ee!"

Lorraine and Julia were later joined by Ruth Swinscombe, a young woman with great character, a hard worker but one of those people who are not at their best first thing of a morning. No one normally spoke to Ruth until at least coffee break, except "shouting for Ruth to get-up" in the morning was a pastime enjoyed by all. On tour Ruth particularly hated the extra early call on 'build-up' mornings, when the circus was arriving in a new town and the tents were erected. I do however remember one morning when to surprise us Ruth awoke on 'build-up' long before us all, which was a great surprise especially as it had been a long drive the night before from the previous town and none of us had got much sleep. It was a bigger surprise for Ruth to learn that the lorry transporting the stable tents had broken down en route, and we were delayed by several hours, all of us having to listen to a very annoyed Ruth!

It was with Ruth that I once had a very memorable horse ride one sunny Sunday afternoon at the Farm. Ruth sat astride Cherif, a handsome Arab stallion, one of Mary's liberty troupe, and I rode Amber the palamino high school horse.

We set off at a gentle trot, down the tree lined avenue towards the village of Over Wallop. We passed an old couple out for their Sunday constitutional and we bade them a pleasant "Good afternoon". A little further down the lane, a man suddenly emerged from out of a clump of bushes where he had hitherto been concealed. As he leapt out he startled both Ruth and I and the horses. Our two mounts decided that the safest plan of action was to head straight back home and they bolted back towards the Farm. Nothing Ruth or I could do would stop them, and in fact they panicked each other. The faster one ran, the other would try to outdo his partner, running faster still. We charged down on the old couple who we had passed earlier and they both had to dive in the verge to escape the thundering hooves. For some reason all I could think of saying was "Look-out. Indians!" which I screamed at the top of my voice. The two animals cantered and galloped their way, coming to rest only when they reached the gates of the Farm, puffing and panting. Ruth and I dismounted and led them back to their stalls, deciding against continuing with our outing.

The 1977 tour of the Gerry Cottle — Mary Chipperfield circus, taught me a great deal. It gave me my first taste of the sawdust life and I was at *last* a circus person. The tour took in eight south coast towns, beginning with Weymouth, and ending up in London, playing in several of the parks within the capital. I was very happy to be one of the 'caravan folk' and with a friendly company of artistes, and all the animals surrounding me I could not have wished for more. Towards the end of the season however, I became ill with a chest complaint that had plagued me since childhood. I had also damaged my hand after an earlier accident with the Yak, who I was leading from the stables out to a corner of the circus lot where he could graze on some lush grass.

In his eagerness to rush over to the grass he had tossed his head as I was about to clip his lead to his head collar. This resulted in the spring clip on the lead going through the fleshy part of my hand on to the collar. In the confusion the animal bolted with the clip embedded in my hand. It was extremely painful and I had to run alongside the Yak to prevent the clip from ripping through my hand.

Eventually I was able to summon Lorraine who managed to free me and I ran to Mary's wagon holding a flapping piece of flesh together as best I could. Mary nearly fainted when she saw me as I had forgotten how she hated the sight of blood, especially anyone elses.

She actually closed the door of her trailer on me as I approached, shouting from the other side that she would take me to hospital as long as I could hide the hand from her view! Eventually she drove me to hospital, my hand hidden inside a bucket. I had 20 stitches which were sewn without any anaesthetic — very painful.

That hand had actually come into an earlier dose of pain when I

Peter the Yak.
(David Jamieson)

had jammed it inside the tiger's cage whilst closing a shutter, which separated the animals at feeding time. Mary came to my rescue again trying desperately to free my hand which had slid through with the shutter, and try to stop an inquisitive Bengal tiger from sniffing what would have been a tasty hors d'oeuvre! Luckily on this occasion there was no blood to be seen, otherwise I doubt whether or not Mary would have come to my aid. It seems odd that a woman who is undoubtedly very brave should be horrified at the sight of blood. I can remember once, how during a performance she nicked her finger on a prop whilst showing her tigers. The finger began to bleed and she walked to the cage door and quickly summoned a plaster. Afterwards Ringmaster Chris Barltrop enquired if the plaster was to hide the blood from the tigers eyes in case they became excited.

"Not at all" replied the intrepid tiger trainer, "it was purely because if I had seen the blood I'd have fainted!"

Apart from the physical injuries, I felt quite ill and needed time to recuperate. I did not want to leave the circus, but at the same time, it was clear to me that I was not fulfilling the job to the best of my abilities. I had a long chat with Mary, whom I had got to know quite well over the past few months. Being her tiger groom, responsible for feeding, cleaning and general care of her group of six Bengal tigers, I had spent a lot of time with her, as it was only the two of us that had any dealings with the big cats. Mary informed me that my work load could be split evenly amongst the other staff (which I felt would not please them — Hibling would be in their bad books) and if I felt it best I leave, then I should. Shortly after I had returned home to my parent's house I received a letter from Mary and Roger saying a job would be available for me when I was fully fit and recovered.

In fact it would not be all that long before I was back with Mary Chipperfield, and since then I have worked for, and with her over a period of many years. I am very pleased to say that Mary and I have long since progressed from 'employer' and 'employee', and I now regard her and her husband Roger as very good friends. As will be seen later on in this book, it was Mary who was responsible for some of my biggest breaks in circus and I shall always be indebted to her.

After I returned home, I was approached by the Swiss "Flippershow" with regards the sealion job. I was very tempted on three accounts, firstly the opportunity to visit Switzerland, secondly my colleague from Dolphinarium days, Mandy Moore was also going to work on the show, and thirdly the sealion job meant work in front of the spotlight and not behind the scenes! I was, I felt ready to take the Swiss public by storm and was soon on an aeroplane bound for Zurich.

Now, almost a year later Mandy and I were on our way home again. We were leaving Switzerland with mixed feelings. We both had grown very fond of the country, its cleanliness, freshness, and above all the overwhelming beauty had made a great impression on us. We had found some reserve at first from our Swiss workmates and neighbours, who were slightly wary of the two 'Englanders' at first. It seems to me that on the whole, the Swiss are an incredibly polite nation, but have a natural reserve and slight suspicion of foreigners. It took time before we were accepted as anything but strangers, yet once inside a Swiss home, the hospitality and generosity was endless.

More than anything the two of us would miss 'our' animals, the sealions and dolphins. It is not uncommon for people who work with animals that they do not own to begin to regard them as their own personal property. This can, and often does lead to disputes with the real owners of the animal, especially if a decision is being made regarding the welfare of the animal, with which the keeper disagrees. It is essential that anyone who owns animals and employs staff to care for them should work closely and consult their employees. This not only applies to circuses but also to animals cared for in zoos, on farms, stables and even with pets in the home. In all cases such mutual 'working together' can only benefit the animals.

However, for whatever reason, it is always hard for keepers to say "farewell" to animals that are either being sold, or are being left behind.

I had plenty of time to think about this as the aeroplane flew high over the Swiss mountain ranges and made its way over the English

Channel followed by the gardens and fields of southern England. I was basically optimistic and was very much looking forward to returning to the farm at Over Wallop, to seeing old friends both human and animal but most of all to meeting the chimpanzees.

I wondered how the chimps would take to me and I to them. It is most important for anyone working with animals to develop a close affinity with the particular species he or she is involved with. It is pointless to embark on all the hard work that goes hand in hand with animal keeping if you feel little for the animal with which you are working. Most people who work with animals in circuses (and for that matter anywhere else) do so for modest financial rewards, working all hours. Any reward comes from the companionship and affection they have with their charges. Interestingly enough Mandy was soon to demonstrate this point. Having spent all her working life so far with marine mammals, she found it hard to adjust to spending her time with horses, ponies, zebras and llamas which Mary had given her to groom in the circus. After trying for a few months she had to admit that her and horses had little in common so she left to find work with animals she felt more at home with. Mandy was unable to find animal work for quite sometime and in fact spent sometime as a matron in a boarding school (which I found a surprise, but evidently she was good at her job, though I wonder if she had the children jumping through hoops for little pieces of herring!) Today she is the manageress of a dolphinarium in one of Britain's best safari parks near Liverpool.

Mandy and David with zebra 'Humbug' and zebroid 'Bijou'. (David Jamieson)

Humbug and Bijou relaxing in the Wallop sunshine.

(*David Jamieson*)

It was a dark and windy night when a lorry, which had driven over from Longleat Safari Park, pulled up at the big red gates at the entrance to the Farm, as all staff affectionately refer to the training headquarters of Mary Chipperfield. Inside the vehicle were two large travelling crates. From inside of one came loud, complaining noises from someone obviously annoyed at being kept up so late. From inside the other all was quiet and calm. I was to learn later that Fred could sleep through anything. As I assisted with the unloading I caught my first glimpse of the two individuals who were to play a large part in my life over the next four years. The two hairy inmates of the crates stared at me with deep, enquiring hazel brown eyes. They gave me the once-over, then settled down into the warm straw, where sleep would soon find them. Fred and Betsy had arrived.

As it was so late and the chimps were obviously tired, we decided to leave them where they were for the night and transfer them to their living quarters the following morning. I gave them both a drink of warm milk, and sat talking to them for a while, but they were so sleepy that I soon left them. As I reached the door of the barn and turned out the light I heard a soft hooting noise from the crate in which Betsy slept. I christened it her "goodnight" noise as it was only at this time of day did she ever make such a sound, and without fail, she bade me goodnight, every night, all the time I knew her.

Chapter 2

Fred, Betsy, Joey and Anna!

In the morning I awoke early and before anyone else had stirred I went down into the stable block to wake my new charges. They were fast asleep and I greeted them with a warm drink of tea, complete with sugar. They drunk steadily, staring all the while at me, studying me very closely.

Before coming to the Farm they had lived most of their lives at Longleat Safari Park and Mary apart, almost everyone at the Farm was new to them.

They were about four years old and about three foot high. They had both been hand-reared, for various reasons so were used to human company. Fred had especially been a regular visitor to 'The Pheasantry', the house Mary occupies when working at Longleat. He had already become a major celebrity having appeared on a few TV programmes with Mary and made some personal appearances at Fetes, opening stores etc. Both animals had been taught their ABC by Mary. By this I mean a few basic tricks and commands, elementary training akin to what dog owners would teach their pets.

This was our first contact, and I hoped that we would get on all right together. It would be impossible for me to teach them anything if they failed to respond to me favourably; a working relationship with any animal has to have mutual respect.

They finished their tea and politely handed their mugs back to me through the bars of the travelling crate. They looked at me as if to say "Come on then, what's next?" I wanted to transfer them to their living quarters so I opened the door of the crate containing Fred and slipped a collar and lead over his head. He grunted and greeted me as he came out. I felt encouraged. He stepped up to me and gave me a firm, if wet, kiss. I was to learn later that Fred would kiss anyone, and anything, but on that particular morning I felt very honoured indeed. I had thought of moving the two animals separately, but did not want them to panic because of the strange surroundings and being with someone they did not know. I hung firmly onto Fred's lead while I found a collar for Betsy. She slipped out of her crate, but did not greet me, Betsy preferring to get to know someone before showing any sign of affection. She was happy to hold my hand though as I led the two of them to their new home.

Chimps are very inquisitive and they do not miss a thing. I watched the two of them as they surveyed the stables around them. The chimps new quarters were situated in the number two stable block which housed some of the horses and the odd camel or two. It also

Stables at Wallop with the odd camel.
(David Jamieson)

contained a practise ring, opposite which was the chimps' cage. From this viewpoint the chimps could survey a wide range of activities. In later weeks, many a time Mary or Margaret would spend hours trying to coax a horse or camel into a new position only to have the patient training session ruined by a sudden loud scream or hoot from Fred or Betsy, sending the animals in the ring scurrying in all directions. The chimps would be very pleased with the result of their actions and I would be summoned quickly and asked in no uncertain terms, to remove the culprits. I would normally take the chimps on a stroll around the Farm, pretending to scold them, but secretly amused at the chaos the two had caused. Back in the ring Mary or Margaret would attempt to salvage the training session. For the most part the chimps would behave very well when other animals were in the practise ring. They would sit huddled together on a box or branch in their cage and watch the training session intently, commenting quietly on the progress in the ring.

I sat with the chimps in their new cage and gave them a breakfast of apples and bananas. Mary entered the stable and earned a huge scream of recognition from both chimps, who left their breakfast and rushed over to see her, panting and hooting excitedly. Chimps never forget people they like, even if their acquaintance with them has been relatively short, and will always greet their reappearance with loud joyous screams. Mary fussed the two animals, reprimanded me a little

Author with Fred and Betsy. *(Author's collection)*

for having transferred the chimps on my own as they might not have reacted well to me and I should have waited for her. As it was I think she was pleased with their response to me as it augered well for the future.

The stables were now coming to life, and I left the chimps to assist with the feeding and mucking-out of the horses, before going off to breakfast happy that round one in my relationship with the chimps had gone so well. The sun was shining as I reached my caravan, although the early hour meant there was still a slight chill in the air. I turned on the radio, and prepared my usual breakfast of toast and marmalade and gazed out of the window which looked out over the beautiful Hampshire countryside in which the Farm nestled.

The Farm consisted of a large practise shed which contained two full size rings, one for the training of the horses, elephants, camels etc, and the other with a caged arena built for the practise of wild animals. Nearby were several stable blocks, with, as already mentioned, one of them also having a practise ring. There were many large purpose-built enclosures for the lions, tigers and bears, tack and feed stores, sheds for the storage of equipment, such as circus Big Tops and seating. Large and small fields surrounded the Farm in which the animals could graze and there was also ample parking space for caravans and other vehicles.

Mary Chipperfield in the practise cage with one of her Bengal tigers.
(David Jamieson)

The Farm was completed by two cottages. Mary lived in one, although nine times out of ten she would be found in her mobile home, used when touring and which was parked alongside. The other was occupied by Rona Brown and her family. At the time Rona, apart from her other duties, also acted as caretaker for the Farm. Rona and I were involved in an episode concerning two deliquent Shetland ponies that could have ended up in a disaster.

The Farm is bordered by Army property on three sides — strictly out of bounds. These vast areas are used for army manoeuvres, and every so often the military explode an arsenal of weapons. These periodical explosions often rocked the Farm, but interestingly enough, although the human inhabitants often jumped out of their skins, the animals seemed to remain oblivious of the noise.

The fields surrounding the Farm were the subject of rumours, especially pub lunch time rumours. It was often suggested that the fields were mined. This was not much comfort when, late one evening, Dimple and Cognac, two self-willed ponies, broke out of the paddock in which they were grazing and headed with all the determination of lemmings on a suicidal run to the Army property. Rona raised the alarm and the two of us set off in a battered Landrover in hot pursuit. We soon lost sight of them, even though both ponies were snowy-white. It was getting dark but we had no alternative but to head for the army ranges, both praying that the mines were no more than figments of beery imaginations, produced in gossip at the White Hart. Even so, we picked our way very carefully, first in the Landrover and then on foot.

Several hours were spent searching for the runaways, who by now were being christened everything under the sun. After a further hour of fruitless search we headed back via the village to the Farm for reinforcements. As we entered the village we drove past a smallholding and spotted a couple of ponies grazing with a few pigs. Rona murmured as we passed how they resembled Dimple and Cognac. I stopped the Landrover and reversed. On closer inspection it turned out that the two animals grazing away, without a care in the world were in fact the two circus ponies! Apparently, within a short time of their departure from the Farm they had doubled back on themselves, somehow avoiding being spotted by Brown & Hibling, and trotted up through the village. The owner of the smallholding had rounded them up and put them in his paddock where they had been all the time we had been expecting to be blown sky high.

We took the ponies home and rewarded ourselves afterwards with a few drinks at the White Hart where we added fuel to the rumours about the mines. After all, it would make us seem very brave indeed if they were true! As we share the same sense of humour, working with Rona has always been fun and whenever we are together on a job, no matter how tiring or awkward, we always manage to have a laugh or two.

As mentioned earlier, Rona was an expert animal trainer for animals used in films, and Mary's animals were in constant demand for film and television productions, quite apart from her circus activities. Subsequently there was always a huge variety of animals at her Hampshire farm. When I arrived there in the autumn of 1978 the collection included the chimps, several monkeys, African and Indian elephants, eland, zebra, zebroid (a beautiful cross between zebra and palamino), giraffe, llamas, hippo, Guanacos camels, kangeroos, lions, tigers, leopards, bears, pelicans, yak, cattle, Highland bull, horses, including the troupe of twelve matched Arab stallions, ponies and a whole host of dogs of all shapes and sizes.

The daily routine at the Farm began with the feeding and mucking-out of all the animals at approximately 7.30 am. With almost a hundred animals there were a lot of beds to clean! The whole operation took about an hour, after which the staff took breakfast themselves. The smell of freshly made coffee, toast and sizzling bacon would waft from the two cottages and half a dozen or so caravans. Breakfast never tastes so good as when it follows an hour's labour. Although I was chiefly responsible for the chimps, I was expected to help out with other animals and I too was involved with the early morning chores.

After breakfast it was back to work and a long day was ahead of all

Jock the Highland bull. (David Jamieson)

One of Mary Chipperfields giraffes. (David Jamieson)

of us. Jimmy Chipperfield's Circus World was going to feature one of the largest collections of animals to be seen on a British circus for many years and so the autumn of 1978 was a very busy time. Both practise rings were busy from morn till night with either Mary, or sister Margaret supervising training/rehearsals. There was also a steady stream of animals going to and fro between the paddocks for exercise and grazing. The horses, zebras and ponies had to be meticulously groomed each day, and the elephants, camels and llamas also received a daily wash and brush up, an elephant's toilet being particularly time-consuming!

The whole Farm took on an air of organised chaos, but each member of staff sticking rigidly to his or her routine ensured that all the work was done. Training sessions would continue throughout the morning, stopping only once for a coffee break. Just before we took our lunch all the animals would be given a drink, and something to eat, hay nets filled and so on. After lunch, more rehearsals until about five o'clock when the animals' evening feeds were administered. A mountain of horse pelletts, bran, flake maize, linseed cake, oats, sugar beet, fruit, vegetables, bread, fish, and meat was consumed by the various animals daily. Individuals required special vitamins and minerals while many of the animals had little likes and dislikes that had to be pampered to. For instance Jarro, an old Lippizaner stallion that was semi-retired, would only eat his hay if it was slightly damp. Being of a quite considerable age it was no doubt easier to digest it

Jimmy Chipperfield with Charles (father of Fred). *(David Jamieson)*

that way. However, it was not permissible as far as he was concerned, for anyone else to dampen the hay for him in advance. Only he knew how dry or damp it should be. An extra bucket of water had to be provided in his stable to allow him to dunk his hay at leisure!

It was bedlam for a time as the meals were being prepared. A symphony of deafening roars, braying, screeching, trumpeting and bleating coming from the diners was quite an experience. After peace had descended, and the animals had all received their feeds we had a break before returning to start bedding the animals down for the night. Mary and Margaret might do a little extra training with individual animals or perhaps ride one of the horses. Later on in the evening all the animals were watered a final time, although many of the stables were fitted with automatic water dispensers which enabled the animals to drink whenever they pleased. Hay nets were re-filled for the horses to ensure no one went hungry during the night.

Mary and Margaret worked as hard as the rest of us and did not confine their duties to training. They took their turn on stable watch, keeping an eye and ear open to ensure the animals were all right during the night hours.

One of the animals under my care was Sahara another young giraffe, who was a very gentle and inquisitive young animal. He had performed a very simple routine in an act entitled 'Safari Spectacular' with the yak, Highland bull, five camels, assorted llamas, Guanaco

Sahara the giraffe with Margaret Chipperfield. (David Jamieson)

camel and an eland working with him. Sahara was required to weave in and out of the camels and cattle, in a figure of eight, providing the highlight of the animal tableaux.

Sahara had been halter trained in a similar manner to horses and was led round the Farm on a long lead each day, tempted all the while with a bucket of succulent titbits. From here it was a short step, or in a giraffe's case a long step, to leading him to the practise shed, being walked around an empty ring to familiarise him with his future routine. After awhile he was led in the figure of eight around pedestals, minus the camels and cattle standing on them. He was accustomed to the other animals as his large pen was within sight of the cattle and camels. Therefore he was not alarmed when he entered the practise shed one morning and saw them standing on the pedestals he was expected to walk round.

The cattle and camels had themselves been taught their part of the act at an earlier stage, and they were not alarmed at the giraffe's presence, he too being a familiar sight. Sahara was popular with most of the animals and staff, although he was not high on the list of favourites as far as Fred and Betsy were concerned. Betsy in particular would dismiss any overtures of friendship with an ungracious swipe of her hand and an array of rude noises.

Whilst performing in the circus Sahara would inspect members of the audience sitting in the front row, often stealing popcorn or candy floss from an unsuspecting member of the public. His normal diet was a twice-daily mixture of oats, bran, horse 'nuts' (a special concentrated food manufactured for horses), sugar beet, linseed cake, flake maize, fruit and vegetables plus as much hay as he wished. He also received a liberal supply of vitamins and minerals, and during the winter he used to have his water supply heated slightly. Sahara was always very grateful to whoever delivered his meals and would give his providers a big wet kiss with his long black tongue to show his appreciation! He was an incredibly tame animal, even allowing us to groom him and to oil and clean his hooves. Handling Sahara was a job that required great patience and a calm, quiet approach, unlike the chimps who enjoyed a far more boisterous and noisy daily routine.

Training the chimps for their circus work began straight away. Throughout the tuition of the chimps I received guidance and advice from Mary, although she left me pretty much to my own devices. She knew that for the act to take shape it would be essential that I found my own level of relationship with the animals. Our working together would have to stem from mutual co-operation without too much interference from outside, especially from another trainer. However, I realised that Mary would be 'keeping an eye' on proceedings if only for the animals' sakes! Still, the fact that she had confidence in my training abilities was a big morale booster.

I found out that the best way to approach training with the chimps was a 'little and often' technique, holding short sessions two or three times a day, lasting no longer than 15 minutes. I found that if I increased the duration of these sessions Fred and Betsy became bored and restless, failing to concentrate. Whenever Chipperfields work chimps (or indeed any other animals) they have a special 'rest' clause written into a contract thereby ensuring the animals are never worked too long at any one stretch. This prevents the animal becoming tired or over-worked as well as keeping the situation fresh and interesting for the animal, who might otherwise become bored with the whole affair and completely refuse to work.

Fred and Betsy had already learnt to sit still on a seat, which is one of the most important lessons taught to most circus animals. It also gives an animal great confidence, knowing he or she has their own 'special' place on which to sit as they enter the ring. This makes an animal feel secure and it is essential that the position of the seat is not altered. This arrangement was a great help to me later when the chimps worked in venues other than the circus ring. When appearing on theatre stages, cabaret floors, and later on an ice rink, no matter how strange the venue or building the chimps would recognise *their* seats, and feel 'at home'.

This situation of having one's own chair is frequently seen in human situations — how often are children told not to sit in dad's place at the dining table? In school too, children feel secure and better prepared for lessons when having their own desk and stool with which they are familiar.

All the routines that the chimps performed started and ended with leaving and returning to their place. One of the first commands taught to them was "Place". If the chimps ever left their place during training or performance without being told to, they were reprimanded. By this I do not mean that they were physically beaten! Normally a vocal telling off, was more than adequate. They hated me shouting at them, and they would return quickly to their seats, usually sulking and realising they had committed one of the worst sins possible.

Occasionally I did smack the chimps if they had been exceptionally naughty. Although I am likely to be criticised for doing so, I do not see any difference between my 'clipping the chimps round the ear', and a parent smacking a disobedient child. Certainly, I wounded their pride but nothing I could administer would compare with the fearful blows the chimps would deliver to one another when *playing* together, let alone if they should ever come to blows when squabbling amongst themselves! Many a time a visitor to the Farm has heard a noise that sounded like a murder being committed and having to be reassured it was only the chimps — enjoying themselves!

Nine times out of ten however, a mere look of disapproval from me was enough to quell any riotous behaviour.

As Fred and Betsy got older it was felt safer to have them wear a light collar and lead during performances. No animal is infallable and if their concentration ever wandered, they might easily have been attracted to something outside the ring and ambled off to investigate. With a young animal there is not too much to worry about, but an adult chimp is potentially very dangerous being immensely strong and equipped with strong teeth that can inflict a bite far worse than that of a leopard. Many people cannot comprehend this, and regard chimpanzees as harmless. Although I would not advocate the opposite, my chimps having loving personalities and were adored by many people, but they were like all chimps, very excitable and unpredictable. It was this uncertainty that meant they could not be trusted completely with members of the public.

When performing with the chimps I had an assistant to help me in the ring. They would keep an eye on the animals, especially on those unoccupied, while I was in another part of the ring working with a chimp performing a solo trick. The assistant had to be someone the chimps new and trusted, and also someone who was very alert. The chimps soon learnt how to unclip their leads, especially Betsy, who would constantly check to see if the assistant was awake by unclipping herself, then handing the lead to them, with a very self-satisfied and smug expression.

I had a variety of assistants whilst working the chimps, with Margaret Chipperfield acting in this capacity for the first tour, bringing her animal know-how to the act as well as a touch of glamour.

The chimps' natural abilities of balancing and leaping were capitalised on for the act, Betsy learned to walk on a large ball, projecting it along a see saw apparatus, and also learned a tightrope sequence. Both these tricks were rehearsed with Betsy holding firmly onto me until she got the hang of things and gained control of her balance. She learned to walk on her hands, which necessitated me holding her legs in wheelbarrow fashion with her supporting herself on her hands, as we walked along. It was several months before her muscles grew stronger and she could walk along. At first I held her feet lightly with my fingers to sustain her balance, then eventually she could balance without any assistance from me whatsoever.

She also jumped hurdles of various heights with confidence while Fred, the natural comic, would follow this by running underneath the hurdles instead of jumping them. Anna later inherited this trick from him and with her performing the trick it became a showstopper — especially when she bothered to perform it on the right cue from me instead of when she felt the time was right!

I made the great mistake in the early months of training by rewarding the chimps with titbits. Horses and elephants will gratefully accept a succulent morsel as a reward for a trick well executed, and will graciously accept that nothing will be given for a trick not up to scratch. On the other hand the chimps seemed to feel they had a perfect right to expect something after everything they did, no matter how good, bad or indifferent their attitude was to the trick being taught! If no reward was forthcoming all hell broke loose and the chimps had a temper tantrum. I soon substituted vocal praise for food as a reward saving any titbits till the training session was over.

That winter the act gradually took shape, with the chimps learning quite an extensive routine. I, for my part learnt new things daily about the chimps. Fred and Betsy began to accept me as their adopted father/teacher and soon had total trust in me. As the weeks sped by I became familiar with their individual idiosyncrasies and was able to use them as aids during training. Both chimps were inquisitive, keen to explore new things and surroundings, but Fred more than Betsy enjoyed new challenges. It was Fred who was the better choice when taking a chimp to a film or television studio as he enjoyed the fuss and excitement.

In training Fred was quick to grasp ideas, and learned new tricks at great speed. He was as quick to go off the whole idea and become bored though, his contribution to the act forever being altered to keep him happy. Betsy on the other hand was a plodder. Slower to learn anything she was however solid in her approach to the act, never failing to do what was required of her and above all preferred a daily routine, being quite unimpressed by extra curriculum duties. Betsy liked to stick to the script, whereas Fred was happy to ad-lib.

One morning I wanted to see what Fred would do if I presented him with a toy scooter. After the usual inspection to see if the thing was at all edible he threw it across the ring and trotted back to his seat. I recovered it and called Fred back and showed him how, by pushing, the scooter could be made to move. This, Fred decided was interesting and he copied my movements. Holding firmly onto the handlebars he pushed the scooter along, walking beside it as he did so. We left it there and I praised Fred, telling him what a good boy he was. In the afternoon training period I brought out the scooter, Fred hooted with recognition, rushed over and grabbed it and pushed it along, a little too violently perhaps, but at least he was enthusiastic. We carried on like this for a few days before I decided we ought to start doing this properly and I attempted to show Fred where to put his feet. This was where the trouble started.

Up until now Fred had thought that the scooter was one of the best games I had come up with yet, pushing the thing along was fun and any innovation was a pure waste of our time. He would look very bemused as I firmly held on to his right foot placed on the scooter, and with my other hand I propelled the scooter along, hoping Fred would lend a hand by pushing with his free foot. No such luck, despite my efforts of persuasion, Fred refused to co-operate.

As the days wore on I was getting nowhere, my efforts in manipulating Fred's feet into the right position were only resulting in my appreciation of how a contortionist must feel.

I began to view Fred with suspicion. I started to think that it was not a case of Fred failing to understand what I was asking him to do — there was much more to it than that. All Fred wanted to do was hold the handlebars and walk alongside it. He had decided that this was the correct method of scooter operating and nothing was going to convince him otherwise. I had no alternative but to try to use Betsy as an aide. One afternoon a few days later I produced the scooter and instead of calling Fred over, I called Betsy, much to his chagrin, and we started to play with the scooter. This had the desired effect as Fred threw a tantrum, becoming enraged with jealousy!

I stood my ground and told him in no uncertain terms that if he was not prepared to learn the trick properly I would ask Betsy to do it. I cannot vouch that he understood what I was saying, but he certainly understood what I was getting at! The episode had at least made him pay closer attention to what I was asking him to do with regards the scooter. Within a day or two of my resuming teaching him the trick, he mastered the art of riding the scooter correctly. However, I swear if he could have spoken he would have remarked "if this is what you wanted, why didn't you say so?!", such was his attitude.

When the chimps practised there was plenty of noise and bustle going on around them. A radio was always playing in the practise sheds and people were constantly coming and going. This activity ensured that the chimps would not be alarmed when they made their debut with me in a public performance.

Such a debut was getting closer and in fact it was closer than I imagined. Although the first ever tour of 'Jimmy Chipperfield's Circus World' was not to commence until the spring of 1979, Margaret Chipperfield was taking some animals to appear in a Christmas circus. This was being staged by the Gandey circus family at a sports hall in Bolton, and it was agreed that I should go and assist Margaret with the three elephants, camels and assorted horses that were being presented in the show. The opportunity was also to be used to accustom the chimps to a circus environment, and perhaps work them into the show. At the time, Gandey's circus was not the large outfit that it is today, and having the Chipperfield animals in the show was something of a 'scoop'. The director of the show, Phillip Gandey and his tall, glamorous wife Carol, were delighted to let the chimps appear in the show along with the other acts. We worked during the final week of the three week run and I can remember spending the first two weeks feeling very anxious, hoping the act would go down well.

We provided the chimps with two appealing outfits from a children's outfitters; red and blue romper suits with an appropriate circus elephant motif on the front. I dug out a blue and silver suit in which I had presented the sealion act in Switzerland and Margaret donned a sumptuous blue evening dress. Whilst looking at us before we worked for the first time, I felt that at the very least we looked smart!

During the first couple of weeks of that Christmas season, I was kept very busy helping Margaret with the animals and I rehearsed the chimps at odd intervals during the day. They themselves took great interest in all that was going on, and got very excited at show times when the other animals went to and from the ring. Eventually the debut performance arrived and I stood behind the curtained entrance that hid the performers from the public. I listened to the Ringmaster's announcement that would soon become very familiar,

"Ladies and Gentlemen! Will you welcome Mary Chipperfield's chimpanzees trained *and* presented by Mr David Hibling!"

We were on. That first evening the acts seemed to go by without me even realising it, and in what seemed like seconds we were acknowledging our first applause and making our exit back through the sequined curtains, from which we had entered. The chimps had performed their tricks without putting a foot wrong, and more importantly I had managed to give everyone the right cues. Chimpanzees have a special place in the hearts of circus goers and the Bolton audience on that January night was no exception, they had clapped and cheered, making us feel very welcome.

Gratifying as the audience applause was, I was even more proud of the fact that the other performers in the show had crowded onto a tiny balcony overlooking the sports hall to cheer and clap for the 'new-boys' (and a girl).

The audience reaction at Bolton taught me one vital lesson. It was that chimpanzees in the circus ring are appreciated more for what they are, than for what they actually do. The simple tricks performed received as much applause as did the more complicated ones. I decided to make sure that in future, when constructing a routine with the chimps, I would not lose sight of this fact and make sure that I never sacrificed the animals' natural appeal for the sake of a sensational trick.

The Bolton season over, we returned to the Farm where preparations for the forthcoming tour became more and more hectic as the opening date approached. The circus was opening on a site at Newbury racecourse on 4th April, to be followed by a tour of major cities. This included a summer season in the beautiful old circus building in Great Yarmouth on the Norfolk coast.

Mary decided that a Western flavour should be given to the act with the chimps. I donned cowboy outfits and to make for a sensational entrance to the ring we decided the chimps should ride ponies. It was also decided that a third member should join the act —

Betsy on the tightwire.
(David Jamieson)

Joey a young baboon.

Mary had already taught Fred and Betsy to ride and the rehearsals with the two spotted ponies, Pancho and Zulu went without a hitch. The only problem was stopping Betsy from administering her own reprimands, if the ponies made a mistake in performance or went too fast for her liking!

I wondered though, how the two chimps would react to being joined by Joey, and equally important how would Joey take to us? Joey was a fine looking animal, with his own brand of humour that he obviously felt was wasted on us. In an attempt to give him as much freedom as possible, Joey was tethered on a long light rope at various points all over the Farm, with new areas to explore every day. His favourite pastime was to lay in wait, unseen behind a bush or vehicle, and then leap out and ambush an unsuspecting person or dog that passed by. As most of us were unaware just exactly where Joey was on a particular day, you could guarantee that Joey would surprise several people going about their daily tasks. Not that Joey ever injured anyone, as he was only playing. He was very friendly with other animals too, and played for hours with the dogs that roamed the Farm. Above all he loved to be in the company of camels whom he would groom, and then have a doze between their humps!

Joey had always been very amiable towards me, and was quite undisturbed when I took over the day to day responsibility of caring for him. I did not have to teach him anything new, but just adapt what Mary had already taught him. He would jump hurdles like Betsy, manipulate a seesaw for the two chimps and his piece de resistance was a spectacular front leg walk around the ring curb that borders the sawdust ring. This spectacular feat was taught by asking Joey to jump over a small hand held stick which was then brought up sharply so that his back feet could grab hold of it. Similar to Betsy's hand walk, Joey and Mary would walk along in wheelbarrow style with the baboon supporting himself on the stick. Gradually the weight was transferred to his front and he no longer required the support of the stick. Although it was a relatively easy trick to teach and perform it always drew great applause, as it did look very impressive.

To get the chimps used to Joey, I made a point of keeping him within their sight the whole day. When he first joined in on the chimps' training sessions, this was from a distance but eventually he went in the ring with them. The chimps and Joey actually viewed each other with great indifference. It was obvious that Fred and Betsy would never accept him as a colleague, but it was enough that they accepted his presence in the ring for performances.

Joey was not saddened at the lack of social co-operation, as he seemed to regard the *chimps* as inferior beings. In reality both Fred and Betsy were of superior strength, size and intelligence but this fact escaped Joey, and he was not intimidated by them in the slightest.

Although the three never came to blows in the year they worked together, towards the end of their partnership I did detect an uneasiness between the chimps and Joey. The baboon retired from showbusiness but makes the occasional comeback in a few feature films. Now an adult, Joey is very impressive and is complete with awesome fangs. In his 'retirement' he has been joined by a mate and the pair have become very attached to one another.

To go along with the Western theme I taught the chimps a trick that was to become a great favourite with audiences. The idea was that Margaret and I would indulge in a spot of whip cracking. We would rip some hand held sheets of newspaper to shreds with the whip. Fred and Betsy would then attempt to imitate us, with Fred holding the whip and Betsy the newspaper. Fred would let the whip crack in all directions, leaping up and down and going quite mad. After a short delay Betsy would madly rip the newspaper up with her hands! Whilst it was not in anyway a difficult trick to teach, it was the consequences of being taught the trick that brought difficulties later on. For instance Fred found that the most amusing use of the whip was to aim it at the ring staff (the valiant lads who erect and dismantle props used in performances, under the direction of the Ringmaster). If possible members of the band came in for a whipping, but better still, the Ringmaster himself!

Joey the baboon.
(Author's collection)

Betsy, on the other hand decided that the paper tearing had to be rehearsed at every opportunity and subsequently would spend hours destroying any paper material she could get her hands on. She particularly liked to devastate a cardboard box, and the concession staff would save empty boxes especially for her when we were on tour.

One afternoon, a few weeks before the circus opened at Newbury, I took Fred to a local shopping centre to hand out leaflets advertising the show. When travelling with the circus the task of performing advance publicity for the show often fell on the chimps and myself. Such outings were especially enjoyable for the chimps, who got very spoilt by shoppers and shopkeepers alike, many of them handing out gifts of fruit and the occasional sweet. I never ceased to be amazed at the number of people who took the sudden appearance of a chimp in the centre of their town, completely in their stride, acting as if it was an everyday occurrence.

At Newbury Fred and I made the acquaintance of a young lady, Lyn Long an ex-school teacher who, like so many people, was attracted to the mystique and romance of circus life. She had answered an advertisement for the job of "Publicity assistant" with Circus World. She soon discovered that her duties were not confined to the Publicity department!

As with all circus life, 'mucking in' was the order of the day and Lyn found herself becoming an expert in programme selling, shopping for animal foodstuffs, handling customers at the box office, and battling with the elements during pull-down (the dismantling of the circus, as opposed to build-up — the erection of the tents etc). Any romantic notion people might have about circus life is soon dispelled on a wet pull-down when due to the rain, everything is twice as heavy and everybody is cold and soaked through to the skin. No one is excused from build-up or pull-down on an English circus, and every man, woman and child lends a hand.

Lyn persevered with her work, adopting a cheerful attitude which, matched with great enthusiasm for all she did, won her many friends in the circus, myself included. She was given the chance to air her acting abilities when she acted as stooge in the 'Riding Machine' act that closed the show. In this, members of the public are invited to try to ride a circus horse, emulating trick riders. Amber the Palamino was usually chosen for the act as he entered into the spirit of things and would buck when the would-be riders attempted to kneel up on his back. All the volunteers were attached to a lunge and were perfectly safe, but the sight of them dangling in mid-air after falling off the horse was a great source of delight to the audience, especially the friends or family of the unfortunate rider!

Lyn's task was to be the final volunteer and as a finale to a series of misfortunes that would befall her during her riding attempts, she would lose her skirt revealing an old fashioned pair of bloomers! Such was the aplomb with which Lyn carried out her duties that few in the audience could have suspected she was a stooge, unless they saw through her disguise and recognised her as the lady who had earlier sold them ice-cream. My task in this act was to 'keep-up' the horse, ensuring that he galloped round the ring at a steady pace, not too fast, not too slow. I looked forward to taking part in the act as it was always amusing and as entertaining for us as it was the audience. The 'Riding Machine' is a very old act, dating back hundreds of years, but it never fails to entertain circus goers, and the sight of someone losing their skirt or trousers, one of the world's oldest gags, is always guaranteed to bring a huge howl of laughter.

Lyn had a romance with the circus's excellent drummer Jon de Jonge, which much to everyone's delight continued after the season, with the two eventually getting married. They have since followed successful careers both in and out of the circus. All this was a long way off from Newbury where Fred, Lyn and I were busy handing out leaflets to shoppers, rewarding ourselves with a cream cake and a cup of tea with Fred displaying his usual impeccable table manners. Public interest was steadily growing in the new show, and advance bookings all along the route were very encouraging. At Newbury, the large red Big Top, which formerly, had been used by the Moscow State Circus on a tour of Italy, was built-up a couple of weeks before the Gala opening of the show, to enable rehearsals to take place.

One by one artistes from all over the world were arriving at the Newbury site, many meeting each other for the first time. Others, as often in the world of circus, renewing acquaintances with friends they had made on previous tours with other circuses. The animals too, were arriving daily from the Farm and the travelling stables were filling up and looking very impressive.

The posters proclaimed it as the 'new quality show' and indeed such a comprehensive array of acts and animals had not been seen on a British travelling circus for many years. For the record the show as seen at Newbury featured; The Flying Rochelles, four youngsters from South Africa on the flying trapeze, The Cottrellis, British handbalancers and equilibrists, Duo Roche on the aerial cradle, Noe-Noe and Gary, father and son who contributed the clowning on the show, Brenda Larenty, the ballerina on the tightwire.

Brenda also performed a unique trapeze act devised by Jimmy Chipperfield. For this she performed a skilful routine on a trapeze attached to a long arm, which was propelled by Bunja the elephant slowly walking around the ring. Brenda made her entrance and exit on the back of the elephant. Neville and Pauline performed on high stilts and the animal content included Carl Fischer Jnr presenting five African elephants, Mary Chipperfield with her tigers, Margaret Chipperfield with a liberty group of zebras and spotted ponies, and

Elephants with Carl Fischer Jnr. David assisting in ring doors. *(David Jamieson)*

Margaret and Pedro. *(David Jamieson)*

Gary Stevenson — juggling. *(David Jamieson)*

Willie Cotrelli. *(David Jamieson)*

Brenda Larenty. *(David Jamieson)*

Flying Rochelles. *(David Jamieson)*

Mary with Liberty horses.
(David Jamieson)

Noe-Noe and Gary.
(David Jamieson)

the "exotic act" of camels, cattle, llamas and giraffe. The sisters combined effectively to present high school and liberty horses. (High school being the circus equivalent of dressage riding.) There was a large 'Carousel' finale which involved four large spotted horses (on loan from the Swiss National Circus Knie), a camel, all the Arabian horses, and the show's artistes all forming an impressive tableaux in the ring. There was a large band, excellent lighting, and of course Fred, Betsy, and Joey!

The show opened to great acclaim from both press and public alike, but the Hibling contribution was almost withdrawn at the last minute. Unbeknown to me Jimmy Chipperfield, who due to heavy business commitments, had not seen the chimp act rehearse, suggested it might be wise to omit the act for fear it was not up to scratch. Never having seen me work before, he was naturally anxious about the act's strength and was obviously keen for the opening night of his new show to run without a hitch. However he had enough faith in his daughter Mary's judgement, who insisted that the chimps and I should be included. To his credit, after I had worked on the opening night, he immediately rushed around to the backstage area to congratulate me and the chimps on our performance. To do this he left his guests in the V.I.P. box and I felt very proud and honoured.

A few weeks later, a review of the circus appeared in the World's Fair, the leading newspaper devoted to showmen. It said of the chimps,

". . . . . the other (animal act) being the chimpanzees and baboon shown by David Hibling. David a former circus fan has I believe worked in Switzerland, and this was the first time I had seen him in the ring. Dressed in Western style the act opened with him presenting the chimps riding ponies. The Western theme continued with a shoot-out, one falling 'dead' and some whip cracking. A wire walk, a globe walk up and down a seesaw and jumps over hurdles etc. are other tricks carried out by the chimps who were joined by a baboon which performs a front leg walk around the ring fence and manipulated a seesaw for the chimps.

The act closed with all three riding ponies and jumping poles. The act had originality and novelty and was obviously enjoyed by the audience."

I was indeed proud of the 'Kids'. I am not sure who it was that coined the nickname 'Kids' for Fred and Betsy, but I believe it was the circus's Front of House Manager, Joy Sloan.

Joy, who comes from a long line of famous circus clowns and stiltwalkers, displayed great courage during the first tenting tour of Circus World when Betsy managed to open her cage one day. I happened to be away with Fred on some publicity appearance, and whether or not Betsy was put out by being left behind I do not know, but she set to work with great determination and managed to loosen the wire in front of her quarters, creating a gap through which she squeezed. She was spotted merrily running around the circus site by Anne Fischer, wife of animal trainer Carl, and she alerted Joy. Whatever the publicity appearance was, it caused all the animal trainers to be away from the show, a very rare occurrence and probably the only time on the tour when no trainers were present on the show. Betsy had chosen her moment very carefully.

Joy knew Betsy must return to her quarters, and armed with a banana she assumed an air of confidence and approached Betsy, took hold of her hand and led her back to the chimp wagon. With the help of extra bananas supplied from a distance by Anne, Betsy was persuaded to go back inside. Joy waited with Betsy while a carpenter was fetched to repair the exterior of the cage. By the time Fred and I returned all was quiet and in order.

The fact that Betsy was quite happy to accompany Joy back to the wagon was due largely to Joy's attitude. Outwardly, Joy communicated to Betsy an air of calm authority. Inwardly, I am sure she must have been very nervous, being aware of the potential threat the chimp could pose to a relative stranger. If Joy had panicked and acted hastily she would have upset Betsy and risked being bitten. Also, once Betsy found herself away from her familiar surroundings she no doubt felt insecure, if not a little alarmed and probably welcomed the opportunity to return to her 'home'. This has often been the case when a zoo animal has broken out of its enclosure. After an initial dash and run around they then try to return from whence they came, for after all, it is there where they feel secure and comfortable.

Of course, having said that, there is always an exception to the rule, and such an exception proved to be Joey.

The circus was appearing at Streatham Common in London, and Joey provided one of the most unforgettable episodes of the whole tour. We had finished the act and were returning to the chimp quarters. The chimps went inside, and received their after-show titbit. I was about to put Joey back in his cage when I accidentally let go of his lead and he immediately sped across the common with all the speed of an express train. I followed in hot pursuit, hampered by the fact that I was still in full cowboy costume.

It was a very warm afternoon, and Joey crossed the road and disappeared through the front door of a house which had been left open because of the weather. He went through the hall, into the kitchen and out the backdoor which had also been left open and into the garden. I followed and spotted the runaway in a tree. I called him in what was, I hoped a very persuasive tone, and he came to me, albeit very slowly. He put his hand in mine, I grabbed hold tightly of his lead and started to return to the circus. We went back through the house just as the very startled lady occupant was coming down the staircase. She stopped in sheer amazement as a cowboy holding hands with a baboon dressed as a red Indian strolled past in her home! With her mouth wide open in disbelief, she was glued to the spot. I raised my hat, murmered something about how pleasant the weather was for the time of year, and made an unhurried exit through the door.

The life of anyone involved with a travelling circus is full of dramas and excitement, and I can understand why the nomadic circus life has often been depicted by writers and film directors as a romantic one. As I explained, the romance tends to be overlooked when you are up to your ears in mud and the rain is pelting down, but the sun soon shines again and I never tire of the thrill of waking up each week in a new town or city.

For me, of course, my daily routine would evolve around the 'Kids', Joey, Sahara and the other animals I was involved with. I awake each morning at around 7am and *if* the sun is shining there is nothing quite like waking up on a circus site, especially if the show is playing in a grassy field or a park. Outside the caravan window there is the sight of a magnificent Big Top, with its flags and banners fluttering gently in the breeze, around you are the sounds of animals waking; horses stomping and stamping their hooves impatiently as they realise breakfast is on its way, elephants trumpeting as their keepers warm up their drinking water. The lions and tigers roar as the shutters are removed from the front of their travelling homes, and the younger animals gambol out into the exercise cages to play in the early morning sunshine.

I would make myself a cup of tea, preparing one for the chimps and Joey at the same time. I would also boil a kettle to add to Sahara's drinking water. On tour Sahara slept in a custom-made travelling stable the sight of which must have made many a motorist look twice when on the road. At the circus site a large enclosure was built on to it thus enabling the young giraffe room enough to run around.

After the chimps had breakfasted, I cleaned out their beds, and introduced them to their 'toy for the day'. Each morning the chimps had something new to play with, whether it be a cardboard box, an old car tyre or even a discarded pair of trousers, it would give them hours of fun. It really is amazing what can be done with a couple of cardboard boxes, and the chimps were forever inventing new ways of destruction!

As at the Farm, I would assist Mary and Margaret during the morning with the exercise and rehearsal of the other animals. The horses and elephants would be taken into the ring for practise after breakfast, and if the circus was standing in a park or field, the horses would be lunged or ridden outside. The elephants also had a chance to stroll about the site but animals such as the camels and llamas were not needed for practise. Therefore they would leave the stable tents in the morning and be turned out to graze on the grass. After lunch, all the animals would return to the stables where they would be groomed in preparation for the two shows at 4.45pm and 7.45 pm.

The chimps too, would have a morning stroll each day, stopping off at someone's caravan for a cup of tea. We would practise in the ring, but often, when the weather was warm and sunny we would stay out of the Big Top and work in the open-air. We normally had a picnic lunch and I well remember one delightful picnic at Winchester. The circus site was in the middle of a delightful park, surrounded on three sides by a stream. The chimps spent the entire time bombarding the local duck population with bits of apple and bread with well-aimed shots!

After lunch, whilst I groomed Sahara and gave a hand with the grooming of the horses, which was very hard work, the chimps took a siesta. All of a sudden a whistle blew signalling that it was time to get ready for the show as the doors were about to open and the public were filing into the Big Top.

Like the other animals, the chimps had their main meal after the first show. For the chimps that meant fruit and vegetables of a large variety, bread and jam, eggs, and the odd cake or similar sweet stuff. After the second show they received their last drink for the day, normally a warm milky one. Then they rearranged their straw beds into a warm nest in which they would sleep soundly until I woke them in the morning.

Every moment I could spare, I would read any book about chimps that I could lay my hands on, and would write to people who had worked with apes or studied them, asking for advice. One of the nicest letters I received was from Molly Badham, co-owner of Twycross Zoo, an establishment that has had remarkable success with the breeding of all kinds of primates. Molly also trained the chimps that for many years were featured on the television commercials for tea. She replied to a letter of mine with the advice that the best way to care for chimps was to 'simply love them'. It was sound advice.

The best way of obtaining knowledge about the 'Kids' was simply to watch them as they went about their daily routine of playing and working. I would try as often as I could to sit with them as they rolled about and played, joining in if they asked me to. More often than not they played too rough for my liking! If mock-fighting they thought nothing of biting each other or even tearing out clumps of hair, but chimps are tough. Other times however, we would all sit together and groom one another peacefully. Grooming is very important in chimp society.

They do not look for fleas when they groom one another but normally they look for bits of salt, in a similar vein to a dog licking his owner's hands or legs. It was a great source of relaxation for the chimps and they would love to sit in the sun and run their fingers over each other making a contented sucking noise with their lips. I always felt honoured if the chimps would sit and groom my hair, as it was the surest sign of being accepted as a social equal. Betsy in particular enjoyed grooming, and being groomed. She also had a great passion for spots! If ever she noticed one on somebody she would pant and hoot with excitement and do all in her power to rush over and pick it! Sadly this was not always appreciated by the poor soul who was inflicted by the spot. Betsy's more indelicate habits were not confined to spot-picking. She also adored ear wax, and would endeavour to obtain a daily supply. Alas, she was not always ladylike!

The more time I spent with them the more I realised how individual their characters, likes and dislikes were. Members of the public often enquired, "How do you tell them apart?", which I always found very amusing. Not only did they look different, their whole persona set them apart as distinctly as two human beings. Fred was far the prettier. A rounder face than Betsy, he was the stereotype chimp. Thick glossy black hair bordered his face, which was far 'whiter' than Betsy's.

Betsy was not a beauty by any stretch of the imagination. She had a very freckled and blotchy face, while the hair on her head was thin in common with a lot of chimps who, similar to humans, tend to bald as they grow older. However, what Betsy lacked in looks she made up for in charm. She was very maternal, and often if I felt low or miserable I would sit with Betsy who seemed to understand that I was not happy. Without saying anything, she would sit and cuddle, hoping to comfort. Betsy could be shy with strangers if she felt a little unsure of herself. Fred on the other hand, was bold and very sure of himself. That was probably why he delighted in the chance to be in TV studios or similar, entering whole-heartedly into the spirit of things. Betsy always needed a little reassurance that new experiences were fun, however she could let herself go like the best of chimps, and when happy or excited would match Fred easily with enthusiasm and vocal strength!

It never ceases to amaze me how animals in a circus seem to be aware of different days of the week. All the animals seemed to know the difference between the day the circus got ready to pull out of a town and a normal one. It was not always the same day of the week either. Normally on Circus World we moved on a weekly basis, with the pull-down on a Saturday evening following the final performance. The build-up was on the Sunday morning after travelling through the night to the new destination. However, on occasions when visiting smaller towns, the show would play for two or three days, moving mid-week.

Yet whenever the move occurred the chimps and other animals would sense what was going on, accepting early feeds and making ready to travel. The chimps loved moving and would hoot excitedly at everyone as they went about their preparations for travelling, watching all and sundry with great interest. The pull-down on Circus World did not take long and was normally over and done with in a couple of hours, unless the weather was extremely bad. The Big Top, seating and all the circus equipment would be loaded onto the large lorries. The animals would be carefully installed in their vehicles for travelling, the grooms ensuring they were comfortable and given a supply of food for the journey.

The build-up has most people helping to put the Big Top up, except the animal grooms and trainers. They busily erect the stable tents and pens before unloading the animals and spending time catering for their needs. The area in which the Big Top is erected has already been marked out (normally a week or so in advance of the circus visit) showing the positions for the stakes and the King Poles. These are the main poles from which the tent is suspended.

The stakes are hammered in with sledge-hammers, the King Poles erected and guyed off with heavy wires. The canvas of the tent is made in sections and these are laid out, then laced together with rope lacings. At the base of the King Poles (there normally being four, but sometimes two, or even six or eight) the canvas is attached to bale rings which are hoisted up the poles, pulling up the canvas. At this point of time the side poles are put into place, these having a spike on the end which fits into a ring on the edge of the tent and are tied off to the stakes. As the tent continues to rise, the long quarter poles are taken inside and positioned about two thirds of the way up the tent. They have mushroom heads with holes in, through which ropes attached to the inside of the canvas are passed and tied off to the pole, holding it in place.

Two or three men then pull out the tent by tugging on the side ropes attached to the side poles, while another man ties it off tightly to the stake. The tent is now ready for the seating, bandstand, ring entrance, and the ring itself to be positioned inside. The side wallings of the tent, and the foyer tent are hung in position and the box office opened for business. The build-up complete, the circus folk can turn their attention to putting their caravans and mobile homes in order. If the build-up has taken place on a Sunday, the rest of the day is usually free for relaxation. In the stables the staff can use the free time for catching up on cleaning tack, the animals indulging in a rest period before the busy week ahead.

Sunday nights on tour were a time for circus folk to get together, perhaps to visit the cinema, the local pub and many a barbecue was held. It must be said however, that many of my Sunday nights were spent at the local launderette catching up on the week's washing, with local housewives marvelling at this young man's collection of odd-sized children's clothes!

Sometimes, I would let the chimps help out on a build-up. Fred proved quite expert in wielding a sledge-hammer and knocking in

Austin Bros. Circus Build-up

(David Jamieson)

Austin Bros. Circus build-up *(David Jamieson)*

Austin Bros. Circus build-up

(David Jamieson)

stakes, saving his best performances for television crews who, more often than not, were on hand to record the proceedings on film.

Circus animals too seem to have an inner clock which lets them know that show time is at hand. One of Mary's ponies, Pancho, an attractive spotted pony that worked in the pony/zebra act, as well as providing a mount for Betsy in our number, went through a visible transformation about half an hour before the circus performance began. He might be grazing, or dozing in his stall, but as soon as the show approached, he would prick his ears forward, arch his back, and paw the ground in anticipation.

There are stories of retired circus animals suddenly going through their old routines in their stables on hearing familiar sounding circus tunes. I am sure Pancho will be one such animal.

Community feeling is very strong in the circus and I often think what joy it would be if the world at large could live like a circus. Of course performers have rows and disagreements, but in the final analysis it is the show that matters above all else, with everyone regardless of colour or creed working for a common goal. Nowhere else in life, except perhaps the ballet, have I found such a unique, uncompetitive harmony and spirit. One only has to see how the competitors behave in the annual Circus World Championships. It is not uncommon to see artistes from one troupe helping to erect the apparatus with another act, with whom they are competing against

Joey riding Pancho (the spotted pony) with Margaret Chipperfield. (David Jamieson)

for the 'world champion' title!

The animals too, are a vital part of the close knit community. They tend to cease to be looked upon as animals, but rather as workmates and friends. Instead of saying "How's the horse/elephant/bear" or whatever, you will more likely hear "How's Pedro/Rani/Harry?". Should an animal fall sick, then there is genuine concern amongst the whole company. I remember one occasion when touring with the Austen Brothers Circus, Fred began to choke on a piece of food. I held him upside down and patted his back, but to no avail. I honestly feared he would choke to death, as whatever was in his throat was not visible. It was a sign of Fred's trust in me that despite his distress he allowed me to put a finger into his mouth. I feared the worst and rushed to get assistance. Someone on the show rang a local vet and informed them a 'dying' chimp was on the way. An acrobat from the show, Carlos Michelli, drove us to the surgery in his car. In his panic, Fred wet himself (and worse!) but Carlos was too concerned about the chimp to care about that.

I was getting very distressed as it was like having a sick child, but just as we approached the street in which the vet worked, Fred produced an enormous belch, which surprised him as much as it did us, and produced a small cabbage stalk, the offending article! We took him to the vet for a quick inspection. He was relieved at not having to perform anything else on the chimp, which he quite rightly viewed as a dangerous animal, and pronounced him fit and well. We returned to the circus to pass on the good news to the other folk.

The vet had been unnerved at the thought of a chimp speeding his way for treatment, as it is not everyday that a town vet has to deal with a chimpanzee. One exception is Bob Cull, a vet from Salisbury in Hampshire, who treats any ailments at Mary's Farm. I think he enjoys the visits to the Farm, finding it a great challenge to deal with exotic animals as opposed to the more normal farm livestock, dogs and cats.

Man's knowledge of exotic animal husbandry has improved beyond all recognition. A vet like Bob Cull, who may have to come into contact with elephants or lions has a wealth of knowledge to assist him. Britain is the home of two of the world's leading exotic animal vets, Andrew Greenwood and his partner David Taylor. Their exploits have been captured on television in the 'One by One' drama series based on the books by David Taylor.

It must still be a shock for an unsuspecting vet to come across a 'wild' animal in his waiting room. Such was the case at Norwich when I was presenting the chimps and bears in Pantomime at the Norwich Theatre Royal. One of the bears, Dallas had a sore eye that needed treatment. I rang a local vet to see if he would visit us. I think he must have thought someone was playing a joke on him as he said to bring the bear to the surgery! Any doubts he had were soon

One of Fred's publicity stints for the Daily Mirror. *(Author's collection)*

dispelled as a rather large Bruin and an out-of-breath trainer, we had just run all the way from the Theatre, appeared in his waiting room. The vet was very calm however and Dallas sat as nonchalantly as any pet poodle on the operating table as the vet examined him and administered the lotion.

The 1979 tour continued and enjoyed very good business, especially in Southampton, Chipperfield's home town, where Jimmy Chipperfield has a beautiful house. The circus was visiting the City at Easter and staged a big circus parade through the town centre. Thousands of people lined the route as marching bands from local organisations led a procession of horses, elephants, camels, clowns and acrobats. It was an amazing sight and equally amazing were the crowds that followed us back to the circus site and sought tickets for the matinée performance. Despite filling the tent as best we could, even to the point of borrowing chairs from artistes' caravans, many hundreds of people were turned away.

It was at Southampton that Fred replaced the presenter of the local television news programme for one evening, and very dapper he looked too, sporting bow tie and glasses for the occasion.

In keeping with our roles as publicists for the circus, Fred, Betsy and I made numerous appearances throughout the tour at fêtes and on many TV chat shows, where Fred usually delighted the camera crews by showing them how to operate their cameras. We also held

Finale (1982) Circus World Championships. (David Jamieson)

tea parties in several large department stores, which were always chaotic, messy affairs to the delight of the visiting children, who perhaps secretly wished they could behave like chimps at their own tea time at home!

Circus World's American Publicity Officer, David Balding was forever organising different publicity stunts for the show, and it was he who had the great idea of having a large inflatable elephant tied to the very top of the Big Top. Unfortunately the giant pink balloon decided to pack its trunk and leave the circus one afternoon as it broke loose from its mooring, and flew away. The runaway did actually give unexpected publicity to the circus, especially as airline pilots at Heathrow were warned to keep a lookout for a large flying pink elephant!

David, a larger than life character, had great enthusiasm for the circus as an art form, and was always good company as he drove the chimps and myself to the various publicity events he had planned.

The chimps would recline in the back of the car, giving the odd regal wave to astonished motorists driving past. I am sure we were almost responsible for several road accidents! Their favourite trick was to suddenly leap to the window when the car pulled up at traffic lights, scaring the life out of fellow drivers or passing pedestrians. The publicity outings were always a pleasant diversion from the daily routine, the chimps as usual being spoilt, especially if we stopped off at a pub on the way home. The chimps were treated to a lemonade with a packet of crisps.

My faith in David's judgement as a publicity officer was only tried on one occasion when he organised a tea party in a London antique shop containing some priceless glassware. I thought he was out of his mind, and told him so frequently on the journey there. I sweated buckets the whole time we were in the store, but luckily Fred and Betsy were on their best behaviour and we returned home with no lawsuit for damages to property against us. I had to endure remarks of "I told you so" from David all the way back to the circus.

Chapter 3

Seaside Circus

It was in 1979 that the Jay family, Jack and son Peter took over management of one of the world's most beautiful circus buildings, the Great Yarmouth Hippodrome. Built in 1908, it is England's only surviving purpose built circus building, the other circus arena, the luxuriant Blackpool Tower Circus being part of a much larger entertainment complex. Since 1983, the Jays have also presented their 'Super Circus' at the Tower building each summer.

The annual Yarmouth summer season has always been well received by holiday-makers and such is the buildings' reputation it is always an honour for an artist to perform there.

In the seventies, whilst the programmes were of solid, high class circus performances and thoroughly enjoyable, they were however felt by many to be 'safe', lacking a certain excitement. In the latter half of the decade the animal content was becoming a little thin in the shows.

Peter and Jack Jay were anxious to install some razzamatazz into the Yarmouth building, but the question was how? Mr. Jay Snr had a wealth of cinema and theatre experience behind him and son Peter had been a successful pop 'star' in the sixties, with his group Peter Jay and the Jaywalkers, but neither were circus impressarios. They decided the best thing to do, until they had gained a little more knowledge of how a circus ticks, was to book a complete programme for the 1979 season, instead of the usual policy of constructing a show made up of separately booked artistes and animal acts. This meant the Jays had to find a circus already operating that would be prepared to come to the Hippodrome for the summer. After touring the country and looking at several tenting shows, the Jays decided to approach Circus World. A deal was struck and the circus made its way slowly but surely to the Norfolk coast.

As the opening of the summer season approached, the Circus World was a buzz with excitement. Just how would the Jay/Chipperfield combination succeed? Would the Yarmouth holiday-makers like the show? Was Peter being too adventurous, booking a tenting circus lock stock and barrel into the famous building? Many feared that the choice of Circus World was a mistake, fearing that in fact the show had too many animals.

However the show was an enormous success, with the circus becoming more than just another, if unique, attraction in the town. It was a veritable tour-de-force, and the Hippodrome was a force to be reckoned with, an audience puller that made the other managements

The Hippodrome, Great Yarmouth. *(Author's collection)*

promoting shows in the town, in theatres and on piers sit up and take note. The show broke all box office records, rewarding Peter Jay for all the enormous effort he had put in to promoting the show. The Jays spent a fortune on the building, with extra stabling being made for the huge collection of animals. For awhile backstage, it seemed that everywhere you looked there were animals, and it was the weight of animals in the programme that was one of the successes of the season, especially Mary's tiger act, presented in her absence by Carl Fischer Jnr. Mary herself had taken animals to Blackpool Tower Circus whilst Margaret was headlining the Yarmouth show for the summer. It was the first time the Hippodrome had featured a cage act in its ring for over 70 years, other than perhaps the odd TV show.

Working at the Hippodrome is a delight, the building being situated right on the seafront enabling the lead animals to be exercised on the beach each morning. The early morning run on the beach is a highlight for many holiday-makers who rise especially early to catch the animals as they frolic on the sand or in the water.

The elephants were especially fond of the sea and would paddle in the salty water under the watchful eye of Carl Fischer Jnr, and his keepers, squealing like little children with delight. The grooms would gallop the horses across the sands whilst the camels would roll about on the sands before dashing back to the building for breakfast. Once they rushed off in the wrong direction and sped towards Wellington

Carl Fischer Jnr. with performing tigers.
(David Jamieson)

Pier, followed by an out of breath collection of grooms and David Balding, who usually joined the animals on the beach. The latter hailed a taxi, and uttered the immortal lines "Follow that Camel!"

Part of the chimps' daily routine was a ride around the town in a little stagecoach pulled by Guinness, a plump little Shetland pony. This was one of the day's highlights. We would begin by trotting along the promenade, stopping off each morning to receive a free ice cream from a benevolent ice-cream vendor. We would slow down to a walking pace as the chimps, myself and whoever of the artistes or staff had joined us on that particular morning, to savour our ices. We could normally time finishing the ice-creams with the arrival of our 'caravan' at a little cafe, stopping off for a coffee. The chimps would have fruit juice and bun with a cake for Guinness. Off again, on the home run, finishing at the St. George's Cafe, opposite the circus building where Christina, the charming Italian Manageress would supply a banana for the chimps, another coffee for the human members on the trip and something tasty for the pony. No wonder the chimps fell over each other in their eagerness to climb aboard the stagecoach each morning!

It was whilst at Yarmouth that Joanna Cottrell, wife of handbalancer Willie, suffered acute embarrassment at the hands of Betsy. Everybody was preparing for the matinée when the peace was disturbed by an ear-piercing scream and they all rushed out of their dressing rooms to see what was happening. In front of the chimp cage stood Joanna minus a skirt, and clown Gary minus his trousers. Any thoughts of accusing Gary of indecently assaulting the lady acrobat were soon dispelled. It was discovered that he had been first on the scene on hearing the scream and in his rush had forgotten his trousers. It did look rather odd at first though, to see the two of them standing there in such a state of undress. Who had taken her skirt off then? None other than a mischievous Betsy of course, who was quicker than any pickpocket. One minute Joanna had been walking along, fully clad in front of the cage and whoosh, a black arm had shot out and away went the skirt. The article of clothing was soon retrieved from the chimp, who was now attempting to fix it to her waist, and order was restored.

Fred caused a sensation too at Yarmouth but in a more spectacular way. Each year in Yarmouth artistes from each of the holiday shows take part in a 'Midnight Matinée', with proceeds going to charity. All the artistes give their services free of charge, with Margaret Chipperfield and I, together with Fred being asked to go along to draw the raffle half way through the show. The show was held that year at Britannia Pier theatre and commenced at 11.30 pm and normally finished in the very early hours of the following morning.

Margaret and I arrived in ample time and settled down in the bar and buffet area provided for the artistes and musicians appearing in the show. There was plenty of free wine available, and Fred, I must admit did have a couple of glasses before his appearance on stage. Whether this affected his performance or not I cannot say, but he certainly provided the audience with an unforgettable exhibition that has gone down in the annals of showbusiness history.

The idea was for Fred to pull tickets out of a large revolving drum and for Margaret, together with comedian Billy Dainty and hypnotist Peter Casson to hand out the prizes. Fred took great delight in spinning the drum and it was with great difficulty that we managed to stop it rotating in order to open the little door in the side and retrieve a ticket.

Fred, disappointed at the sudden stoppage of his new toy, began to revolve the drum before we were ready and before we had shut the little door. Tickets flew everywhere. Fred encouraged by the audience began to grab handfuls of tickets and shower the stage and front row seats by throwing them everywhere!

Somebody, worried about the mess, edged towards the stage with a broom, which was a thoughtful, if somewhat stupid move. Fred grabbed the broom and began to 'sweep' the stage, making a terrible job of it and almost burying the musicians in the orchestra pit, themselves helpless with laughter. Some dancers behind a curtain waiting to perform after the raffle, also began to giggle as they were able to make out what was going on in front. Fred turned his attention on them and began to batter the curtain with the broom! Enough was enough and somehow, with the help of Billy Dainty, who graciously let the chimp upstage him, the raffle resumed and prizes given out.

The following morning in the local newspaper a reporter wrote; "FRED'S DRAW A HIT AT THE MATINEE! It was a bit like the old music hall song 'when father papered the parlour' — but in this case you could not see Fred for tickets! Fred, for anyone who was not at the Midnight Matinee on Friday is one of the chimps from Jimmy Chipperfield's Circus World at the Hippodrome and he came jolly near to stealing the show from a star-studded bill. Someone had the bright (?) idea of letting Fred draw the winning tickets in the raffle during the interval. This he did with aplomb, but unfortunately there were only three prizes. The way Fred went about it gave one the impression that there were about 3,000! Tickets flew everywhere as he warmed to his job!"

Amongst the artistes on the bill that night was TV's top magician Paul Daniels and I imagine he must have been very impressed with Fred's performance as he later invited the chimps to star in one of his shows, more of which later.

The season at Yarmouth finished during the first week of September and the circus resumed its tenting tour. As always, the last night of the Yarmouth season is very special. At the end of the final performance in 1979 the management distributed flowers and gifts to everyone, whilst all the ticket stubs from the season were released from the roof, showering performers and audience alike. For a few moments I wondered if Fred had crept out of his quarters and was masterminding the spectacle.

Within a week the Big Top of the circus had been erected and we were once again playing under canvas. It was sad to leave the Hippodrome, having made friends with the benevolent old building which is steeped in circus history. I little knew then, but I was soon to return and as I write this I am about to embark on my sixth season for Peter Jay. Nonetheless, it was good to be back on the road. The autumn weather was being kind and all around the familiar sights of a touring circus, plus the familiar, exciting smell, a mixture of grass, sawdust, canvas, exotic animals and diesel fuel.

The autumn tour was to culminate in London with a visit to Clapham Common, where it was rumoured a Royal Charity show would take place. It was that autumn too, that Anna came into our lives. Anna was born at Chipperfield's Scottish Safari Park where after a few months, she, like Fred and Betsy had sadly been rejected by her mother. Chimps normally make very good mothers, and it is sad, when as sometimes happens an offspring is rejected. It is always best if a mother will rear her own young as hand rearing a baby animal is very hard work and time consuming. Anna had been reared by Mary at the Blackpool Tower Circus that summer, but she thought it would be a good idea to see if the chimp would mix with Fred and Betsy, and if all went to plan she could join the act.

When Anna arrived on the show, she was without doubt one of the cutest little animals I had ever seen. Still very much a baby she was adorable and not surprisingly, everyone fell in love with her. I soon found out though, that behind the fascade was a very determined young lady with a temper that on occasions even got the better of Fred and Betsy. She was for all that very endearing, and I was thrilled to have her join the 'gang'.

Rearing a baby chimp, is for all intents and purposes similar to rearing a child. They both need all the warmth, love and protection that you can give. A baby chimp has very similar feeding habits to a human baby, and whilst with Mary, Anna had been bottle fed regularly day and night. Chimps are different in one respect, they have very strong vocal chords and woebetide anyone who is late with a feeding bottle as a little chimp will soon let you know he or she is hungry.

Anna was about a year old when she arrived on the circus. She had been weaned and was able to eat solid food but she was still very much a baby and for a few months lived in my caravan with me. Although she had a little playpen of her own in which she also had her sleeping blankets, more often than not she crept into my bed, having accepted me as her new foster dad and felt it only fair that I should have her with me all the time. She hated being out of my sight, which made life very difficult, especially as I kept her away from Fred and Betsy at first, she would throw a tantrum if I put her in her pen and walked away. I had to be firm about this and after awhile she accepted that there were times in the day when I would have to leave her alone for a short while.

Fred and Betsy suspected that someone new was occupying my time. I hesitated in introducing them as Anna was still fairly small and I did not want jealousy to occur. It was important too, that my relationship with Anna was strong before I let her get to know the others. I hoped very much that the three would take to each other as I wanted to retire Joey and work just the chimps the next season. The two older chimps were very suspicious about the way I seemed to be spending a lot of time away from them. Although I struggled to give them as much attention as ever in the wake of Anna'a arrival, the little animal was time-consuming and there was still Joey, Sahara and my other duties occupying parts of my day. I must admit I did spoil everyone a little during the first few weeks of that September, hoping that no one would feel neglected by me giving so much attention to the little chimp.

Like all young animals, Anna was incredibly inquisitive and everything was suitable for her scrutiny. The hustle and bustle of the busy circus was a great source of interest to her, and as I carried her around the site each day it was amusing to see how she was torn between holding on to me tightly for security and wanting desperately to climb down and explore. I introduced her to Sahara who, in his usual gentle manner, bent his long neck and gave Anna a wet kiss. She was not impressed. Anna was however, greatly intrigued with a young tiger that was on the show at the time. The cub thought Anna would make an ideal playmate and rushed at her on their first meeting, which promptly sent the little chimp screaming into my arms. Eventually she lost her wariness of him and began to play rough and tumble games, actually getting the better of the young tiger on most occasions.

After awhile I took Anna to meet the older chimps. Any fears I had about the animals not accepting each other were groundless. Fred and Betsy greeted Anna like a long lost sister, and Betsy's maternal instincts were aroused by the young arrival. The chimps were very excited about the new member of the troupe and gradually, by letting Anna spend more time with the others each day, she left my caravan and moved in with Fred and Betsy.

Anna grew quickly both physically and in character. She was very boisterous and mischievous with much more energy than either Fred or Betsy. Fred soon took on the appearance of a long suffering older brother, especially if Anna indulged in her favourite game of using him as trampoline. I have known him resort to sitting on Anna in an attempt to keep her quiet! The two females became inseparable, and Betsy though still an adolescent herself, took over the role of mother figure, becoming very strict with Anna when she misbehaved. Joey ignored Anna as much as he did the others, preferring his own company, or better still that of the camels who he still had quite a passion for.

Anna's training had began the minute she entered my life. She soon accepted her daily routine, feeding, playtime, rest periods and whilst she lived in the caravan, reluctantly accepted a daily wash with warm water administered with cotton wool. She happily wore T-shirts, sweaters and long socks whenever we ventured out of the warm stables into the cool autumn air.

Author with Anna the chimp and tiger cub. (Author's collection)

She sat in on the daily training sessions in the Big Top. Not required to do anything she would hold on to me piggy back fashion and watch as I put the rest of the family though their paces. The sessions were valuable in accustoming her to the sights and sounds of the circus ring. After awhile she would climb down and amuse herself in the ring, which I allowed as long as she did not interfere with the others as they worked. If she attempted to disrupt a training session a sharp "No!" from me sent her scurrying off to some corner to sulk for a few seconds before rejoining us.

Only after training was over could we all play together in the ring, tumbling over one another in rough games of 'tag'. Tickling was a big part of the play times — all chimps adore being tickled, laughing loudly with delight.

At this stage Anna did not take part in any performances, although she would be on hand as Fred and Betsy were prepared for the show. She watched them as they got dressed, fascinated by the sequins on their costumes. Anna never learnt that sequins were inedible, and we were never able to decorate her costumes with them.

The first step to Anna joining the act began when I introduced her to her own chair which she would use in performances. I positioned it next to Fred and Betsy's chairs during the training sessions and I would place Anna into it immediately we entered the ring just as the others sat down in theirs.

At first she refused to sit in it for more than a few seconds, but she quickly learned that praise would be forthcoming if she sat there. She then began to spend her time sitting down watching everyone else. She soon adopted it as 'her' chair and ran to it each morning. For awhile I was content to have her running around, returning to the chair if and when I asked her to. As she grew older I would tell her "No!" if she got down from the chair without asking. On the odd occasion when she was naughty she would get a smack from me on the bottom, and much to my surprise Fred and Betsy would often administer their own reprimands also!

Once the chair had been adopted by the little chimp it would be an easy step to commence training her the ABC of tricks, but I decided to wait until the winter season was over before attempting to teach her anything too complicated. She would be a little older then and we could debut her talents in the 1980 tour of Circus World.

As Anna progressed in her relationships with me and the 'kids', so the circus progressed on its way to London, and to that Royal Charity show. It had been confirmed that Princess Anne was to visit the circus at a special Gala performance in aid of charity.

The towns en route seem to merge into one, being distinguished only by events or happenings. Ilford for instance, where the wheel of my caravan broke off leaving me stranded for a night as the circus moved on. Chelmsford, where disaster was narrowly diverted when a generator caught fire and one of the ring staff heroically leapt into the cab and drove the vehicle away from a packed Big Top.

Wanstead provided to be one of the most amusing interludes of the whole tour, when Sasha, one of the show's camels whilst out grazing on the 'flats', became untethered and strayed onto a busy highway and promptly lay down, much to the amusement and annoyance of motorists. He refused to budge creating one of the most unusual traffic jams.

After a little coaxing he left the road and went back to the grassy flats, but he still gave us a run around for a half hour before returning to the stables.

My mother was with us on that occasion and I think she quite enjoyed herself running over the flats after the runaway, although she was not the greatest of help. Perhaps not surprisingly, as the huge camel thundered towards her she would step out of its way, despite encouragement from me and other members of staff to stand firm and grab him!

There was an amusing postscript to this little story. Shortly after the camel returned to his stable, a man went to the box office and demanded a statement from the cashier to the effect that the camel had indeed sat down on the road. When asked why, he replied that he had been working late each night that week, and his wife was suspecting that he was having an affair. He had promised to be at home on time that evening, and he felt that he had little chance of convincing his wife that he was late because a camel had sat down in front of his car! He got his statement.

The circus pulled onto Clapham Common, one of London's premier circus sites and for so long the autumn 'home' of Billy Smart's Circus, whose visit to the Common in October and November had been a 'must' for Londoners each year. The popular BBC TV recordings of the circus had always been filmed there.

Since the Smart circus had stopped touring in 1971, it had been Mary Chipperfield who had provided London circus goers with entertainment 'on the common' with visits in 1972, 1974 and now again in 1979. Princess Anne had earlier visited the circus in 1974 and everyone was thrilled to think she had decided to make a return visit.

The atmosphere on the show was electric, the weather appalling! Rain storm after rain storm threatened to turn the whole site into a swamp and trenches had to be dug around the Big Top and stable areas to prevent them from getting wet. Inside the Big Top extra decorations were installed to make everything even more spectacular. A Royal Box was constructed immediately opposite the ring doors, affording the Princess an excellent view. Derek Isles and the band, who had provided stirring music throughout the tour rehearsed new music, and the new acts engaged to supplement the regular programme practised in the ring. All this provided many headaches for our Ringmaster, Chris Barltrop, who was a very efficient artiste. Throughout the tour he had worked hard, not only in his Ringmaster's role, but on countless other tasks ranging from giving radio interviews, to ensuring that water and electrical supplies had been laid on for the circus visit. A Ringmaster's job is very exacting.

To the public he is Master of Ceremonies, talking and introducing the acts to the public. He has to be prepared to handle any difficulty or emergency that may occur in the show. He is in charge of the 'ring staff' the hard working crew whose job it is to erect and dismantle the props used in each performance. He is normally Company Manager, handling any problems an act might have and acting as a vital link between staff and management. He needs to be bilingual, very knowledgeable about all circus acts and animals — and at times very patient!

On hand at the Royal show was Norman Barrett, Britain's premier Ringmaster whose expertise is well known. Norman regularly hosts TV's Circus World Championships and for well over 20 years he had been Ringmaster at the world famous Blackpool Tower Circus. Norman had joined Circus World at Clapham when the Blackpool season had finished as did Mary who had devised some new animal acts during the summer especially for the Royal show. What with the added speciality acts the show was indeed going to be even more spectacular.

Norman Barratt with Mary Chipperfields elephants.
(David Jamieson)

The performance was to be in aid of The Muscular Dystrophy Group of Great Britain, and the Meat Traders and Drovers Benevolent Association.

Princess Anne was to be accompanied by her husband Capt. Mark Phillips GCVO and the show was a sell out, with many celebrities and dignitaries paying a great deal of money for seats, knowing that the charities would benefit.

Roger Cawley had insisted that a number of seats would go on sale at normal prices so that members of the public could share in the excitement of the event.

The Gala day arrived, and as show time approached we were all nervous and excited. We had rehearsed our routines over and over again and Jimmy Chipperfield had instructed us on how to take our bows as we concluded our acts. I kept going through the order in my mind, bow to the right, bow to the left, and a long bow to the Royal Box.

All day the Big Top had been a hive of activity with flowers by the lorry load arriving by the hour and the sweet aroma of fuschias and roses mingled with the familiar sawdust and canvas smells. The Big Top looked beautiful. A couple of hours before the show commenced the 'kids' and I sat down in the deserted tent, save for the ever-present security guards, and we drank in the atmosphere. It was magical.

The tent began to fill slowly, with people from all walks of life coming together to enjoy the Royal occasion. The generators had whirled into life, illuminating the Big Top both inside and out, with thousands of coloured lights. In the caravans the artistes were adding the finishing touches to their make-up, and sorting out their finest 'special occasion' costumes, and no doubt rehearsing those bows. Margaret Chipperfield had found some new red and blue dungarees for the chimps and Joey to wear, and I too had a new blue suit for the occasion. Fred and Betsy seemed to be aware of the excitement generated by all and sundry, and hooted and screeched with excitement as they were dressed.

Only dear old Joey remained impervious to it all, and actually stifled a yawn before we entered the ring.

The band struck up the National Anthem, and all of us backstage knew the magic moment had arrived. Princess Anne, radiant in black and silver had taken her seat in the Royal Box accompanied by the Captain and various members of the Royal household. Jimmy Chipperfield and his lovely wife Rosie, were also in the box providing a commentary on the acts as they performed.

The show commenced and a cavalcade of colour and glamour that is evocative of the circus filled the ring. The artistes hoped that tonight of all nights, they would not drop a juggling club, miss that double somersault, or that their animals would fail to respond to the right cues. Mary and Margaret were especially nervous when it came

During the interval HRH Princess Anne meets Anna the chimp.

(Courtesy Mary Chipperfield Promotions)

to the horse acts, for they knew that the Princess, an accomplished horsewoman would be scrutinising every movement.

As for the chimps, they did not let me down. They performed with gusto, and Betsy spurred on by the extra applause the act seemed to be earning, encouraged everyone by deciding to applaud herself on every trick she performed. Quite out of character.

I swear even Joey put that little extra bit into the hindleg walk, or was it my imagination? My only regret was that Anna was not appearing — what a debut that would have been! However, just before the interval Mary sent word round to the stables that I was to get Anna dressed as she was to be presented to the Princess, during the interval along with the little tiger cub. So, Anna upstaged her colleagues by actually *meeting* Royalty and she was very well behaved, except for taking a nip out of the Princess's bouquet!

After the interval though things got out of hand. One of the new routines that Mary had been rehearsing for the Royal show was a unique double 'Big and Little' routine featuring two large Shire horses, matched with two Shetland ponies, a large bull Asian elephant Maxi, a magnificent tusker, and the equally impressive female African elephant Womba. Two baby African elephants completed the line-up.

The act had been performing for a short while and met huge audience approval, the awe-inspiring spectacle of the draft horses and huge elephants being contrasted with the appeal and charm of the little ponies and baby animals. One feat in particular drew enormous applause, this was when the four larger animals placed their front feet on tubs and the smaller animals encircled them running under their bellies!

This show stopper however almost *did* stop the Royal show. The act went smoothly enough and was almost over, the horses and ponies had exited and the baby elephants were at the ring doors waiting, as the older elephants performed the 'Grand Mount', a traditional end to circus elephant acts. This comprises of one animal walking out of the ring as another follows behind with its front feet resting on the first animal's back. Maxi was resting his feet on Womba's back and Mary had just cued the animals to exit when, for some reason best known to the animal herself, Womba turned round and butted Maxi, forcing him off her back. To the Asian elephant's credit he kept balance and tried in vain to resume his position. Womba was having none of it and hell-bent on mischief she pushed Maxi towards the front seats, the occupants of which were by now vacating them as fast as they could. Maxi had no choice but to fall into the ringside area, over the floral displays. In an attempt to escape the raging female elephant he made his way out of the tent, and directly in front of him stood the Royal Box.

Circus people ran everywhere, Mary and Margaret attempting in vain to halt the two runaways and lure them back into the ring. They were quickly joined by Roger Cawley and Carl Fischer Jnr. David Balding was knocked aside by the fleeing Maxi and lost his spectacles in the fracas.

I had been standing in the ring doors with the baby elephants, and I must admit to being transfixed by the scene for what seemed like an eternity, but was in reality a few seconds. I can recall visually, the horror of seeing the two large animals charging out of the arena towards the Princess, but it seemed to be happening in silence. I expect the band had stopped playing for a few seconds, and most people were too stunned to utter anything. I snapped out of the trance and led the little animals away from the ring, back to the stables fearing that they might attempt to join their elders. They were trumpeting but not unduly alarmed. As we settled in the stables we were suddenly joined by Womba and Maxi, with ears flapping and trumpeting wildly. Hot on their heels were Roger, Carl, Mary, Margaret, and David still minus his glasses.

Apparently the animals had run through the Big Top, missing the Royal Box by inches and made their way via the foyer tent to the outside. Amazingly they did little damage inside the tent, apart from knocking over the odd vacated front row seat. They had not knocked anyone or anything else, not even a pole in the narrow foyer tent had been touched by their huge bulk. Once outside in the cold November night, their excitement had waned and they headed straight for the place where they knew they could find security — their stable.

Back inside the Big Top, Ringmaster Norman Barrett had grabbed the microphone and reassured everyone all was well, not that there had been any panic. The incident had happened so quickly that only those in the direct path of the animals, including a couple of Mayors, had vacated their seats. Although a few people in the stands had stood up ready to flee, the elephants had left the tent before the majority had made any decision to get to their feet. It was rumoured that Capt. Mark Phillips threw himself in front of his wife, but at any rate the Princess made no attempt to move out of her seat, despite justifiable provocation! A very brave lady.

The clowns entered the ring and despite the excitement caused by the charging elephants, 'the show went on' in true show business tradition, and the audience settled back in their seats to enjoy the rest of the performance. The only injury to a member of the public had been to a young lad, who in his excitement, had stood up quickly in the grandstand and fallen off the back of the tiered seating. This in itself caused him no injury, but he had picked himself up and promptly walked into a pole! Luckily he only sustained a black eye.

The show drew to a close with an elaborate finale featuring all the artistes, who then made their way to the foyer tent where we were presented to the Royal couple. The Princess was introduced to us all in turn and showed not the slightest sign of worry at almost having

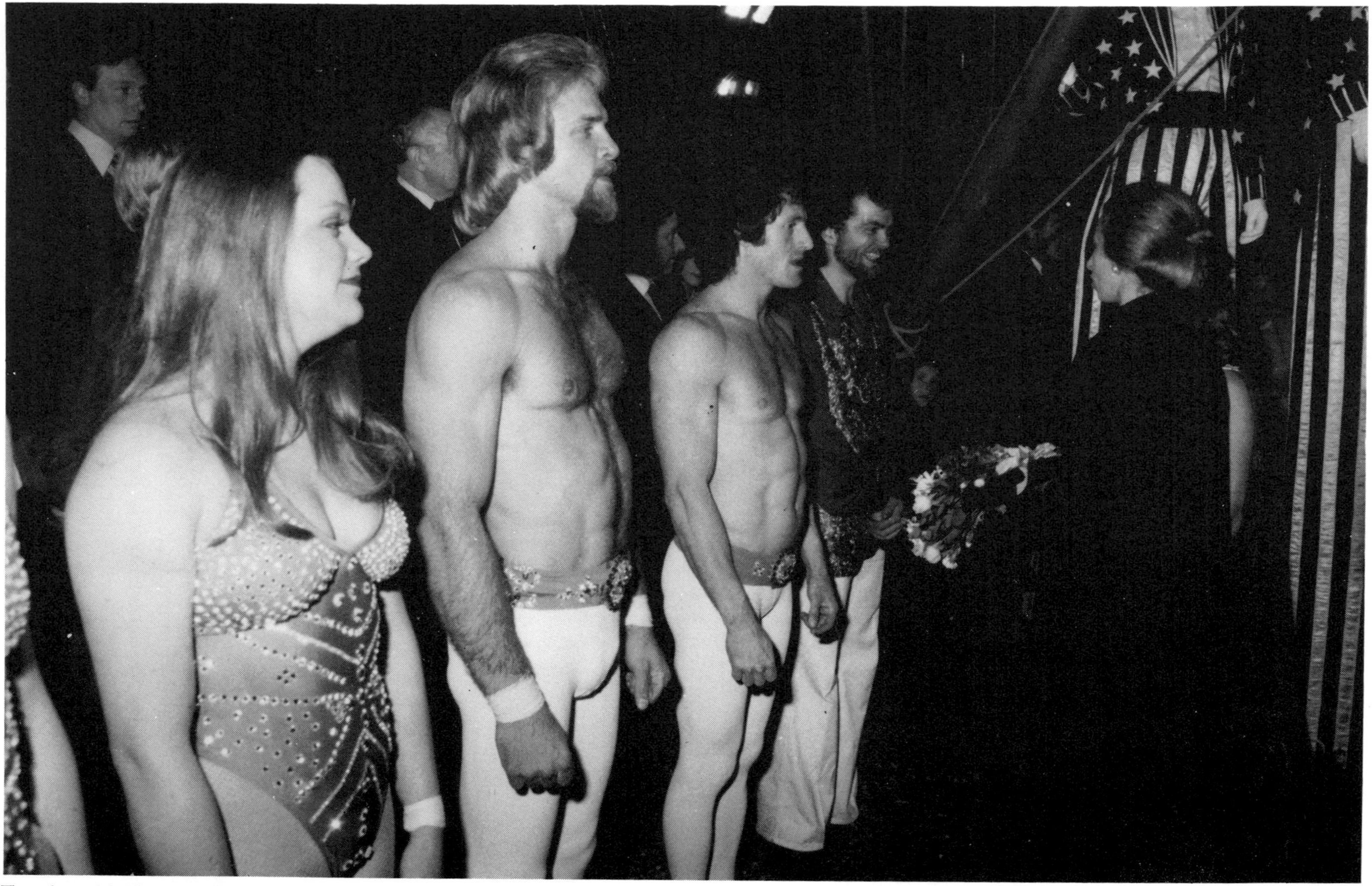

The author and the Flying Rochelles being presented to HRH Princess Anne. *(Mary Chipperfield Promotions)*

been trampled underfoot by an elephant. She obviously had faith in her host's ability to handle animals. I hoped I would not be tongue-tied when I spoke to her. She gave me a radiant smile as I shook hands and she asked how I had started in the circus, and for some unknown reason I replied "Bad Luck!" Much to my relief she just laughed and told me how much she enjoyed the chimp act. The Princess also remarked that she had seen my face constantly cropping up to assist in the other animal acts on the show. A few days later I was able to inform Mary that my work had been given a Royal seal of approval! This was greeted with a characteristic "Never mind that, go and see if they need a hand with mucking out the horses!"

The incident with the elephants had been widely reported, even as far away as Australia. Shortly after the Gala evening, Jimmy Chipperfield received a letter from Buckingham Palace asking him to pass on the Princess' congratulations to all involved with the Gala performance, stating that she had enjoyed herself immensely — even the unplanned excitement!

The event had raised a lot of money for the two charities and everyone seemed pleased. The circus settled down to normal, Womba was forgiven for her atrocious behaviour and the elephants performed without a hitch for the rest of the run.

The 1979 tenting season drew to a close, the final performances being given at Clapham and on an unusually bright November day the circus pulled down. The weather was cheering, Anna and I sat with Joy Sloan drinking tea and watching the first lorries depart from the site. We began talking about the winter. I remarked that judging from the weather it looked like the chances of a 'White Christmas' that year would be very slim. "Probably be another wet one" I muttered.

Little did I know how true that was. The Christmas of 1979 would be a wet one for the circus, a very wet one indeed.

Chapter 4

Bad Tidings at Cardiff

I have always adored Christmas. A romantic soul, I love the Dickensien view of the festival, carol singers, plum puddings, snow falling outside the window and the giving of cards and presents. I would not call myself devoutly religious, although I do believe in God, and I have usually managed to attend a Midnight Mass ceremony each Christmas Eve. Due to my work one thing I have not been able to do as regularly as I would have liked is to attend family get-togethers, which I believe are important, especially at Christmastime. As a child I can remember great family Christmases, the crowning glory of which, for the youngest Hibling at any rate, was the Billy Smart Christmas circus on television following the Queen's speech.

One Yuletide, I shall never forget was the Christmas of 1979, spent with the Jimmy Chipperfield Circus at the Welsh Capital city — Cardiff. From Clapham Common, most of the circus returned briefly to the Wallop farm. Mary was taking groups of animals to the Belle Vue Winter Circus at Manchester, scene of countless Christmas circuses. The bulk of the show however was going to Wales to appear as Jimmy Chipperfield's Christmas Circus World in the Sophia Gardens Pavilion, one of Cardiff's premier concert venues.

As at Yarmouth, Margaret Chipperfield was to headline the show presenting the liberty horses, zebras and ponies, "exotics" with Sahara the giraffe, high school horses and a solo liberty horse, Indian. This was an eye-catching skewbald stallion, that Mary had shown at Blackpool Tower Circus the previous summer. Carl Fischer Jnr. presented the elephants and the new mixed group that Mary had trained, featuring Ikon the African leopard, some young lions and tigers and Harry. He was a large American black bear that had been named after a bruin-like circus drummer. Harry had long been part of the Chipperfield menagerie and had worked in many different groupings of animals for Mary. He was a placid old soul, rather like an elder statesmen, performing what was required of him, yet would not be hurried by anyone, taking his time in everything he did. This even applied to his journey from his living wagon, down through the net 'tunnel' to the ring cage and special allowance had to be made for this. Somebody had to let him out of his wagon nice and early, with plenty of time in hand before the act started. He would make his way slowly along the tunnel, stopping every few feet to pause and have a leisurely sniff. He would eventually wander up to the section of tunnel just behind the curtained ring entrance where he would sit quietly until it was time to enter the ring. Likewise all Harry's tricks were featured early on in the act to allow him time to plod back home, before being joined by the rest of the members of the act.

I was to work the chimps and Joey, still in Western theme, but not with Anna as yet. She would debut in the 1980 production of Circus World. Brenda Larenty returned to the programme to exhibit the two acts she had featured with Circus World on its tour. Newcomers included Gina, a beautiful artiste who performs a unique trapeze routine on a revolving moon-shaped prop. 'Gina in the Moon' is in reality Shirley Fossett, a cousin of Mary and sister to Tommy Fossett who also appeared in the Cardiff production providing his skilled juggling act, and as Grimble, his renowned clowning routine.

Grimble is a hilarious clown creation with touches of genius. The character is a down and out tramp, who is usually in trouble either with the the Ringmaster or a glamorous lady assistant. At Cardiff, Tommy, as Grimble, performed his cod magic routine in which Grimble an aspiring magician attempts to produce a 'duck' from a saucepan during which several eggs are broken in the process. I always made a point of watching the act and would end up in stitches. Grimble enters the ring via the audience, heckling the Ringmaster with shouts of 'Bring on the Dancing guinea-pigs', and other such nonsensical remarks. Grimble is very warm and always enlists the support of the children in the audience during his antics.

He often ends up getting the 'sack' from the Ringmaster and it is always fascinating to see how involved the children get in this industrial dispute!

Tommy is a gifted musician, and ends his act with a musical finale, at Cardiff assisted by his two young sons, christened 'Grandpa' and 'Uncle Fred', they played a rousing version of 'Viva Espania'.

So we had an impressive line-up for the Welsh audiences. Before the show opened Anna and I travelled along to Cardiff to do some publicity organised by the inventive David Balding. Fred, Betsy and Joey travelled back to the Farm for a short holiday where they were looked after by Rona who got on very well with the chimps, especially Fred.

Whilst the others lazed about in Hampshire Anna and I installed ourselves in Cardiff outside the building. Anna was returning to my caravan whilst we did our publicity. David had excelled himself with his advance publicity and we soon found ourselves in a variety of venues and situations, appearing in car showrooms, carpet warehouses, markets and even, on one occasion, disco dancing! This last event went down very well with Anna. Whether it was the coloured lights, or the sight of so many young people gyrating in a very ape-like fashion I am not sure, but Anna thought discos were definitely her scene and she danced and jived with the delighted youngsters.

The Sophia Gardens pavilion was a large barn-like building on two levels with a large stage one end behind and under which were several dressing rooms and store rooms. The circus ring was not installed on the stage because it was felt that more atmosphere could be created by building the ring in the centre of the building and erecting the seating from Circus World's Big Top around it. This was possible as the auditorium had no fixed seating. Outside the pavilion space was tight, and the animal wagons containing the large stable tent for the horses, elephants, giraffe and exotics, and the artistes' equipment and animals deposited their loads and then, because of the lack of space, were returned to the Farm, a fact that was to prove disastrous later on.

The chimps themselves were housed in one of the large rooms behind the stage. Special wooden sleeping dens had been acquired for them to sleep in, and during the day they could run around the room, which being empty they could do no damage! I found some old tyres and with ropes managed to fix them to some beams for their exercise. The chimps were very hardy, having spent so much of their lives out of doors they rarely caught colds. All the same, I was pleased we could install them inside the building.

The Pavilion was situated in a pleasant park not far from the castle and city centre. Alongside the building ran the river Taff which swelled daily during the season as the mild winter produced a great deal of rainfall, both in the city itself and up in the Welsh valleys and hills. The river was forgotten however as the circus opened and installed itself as part of the Cardiff Christmas celebrations.

Christmas Day arrived. I volunteered to stay and look after the animals so that Margaret and other animal grooms could snatch a precious day off with their families. The only other member of the animal staff to stay behind was Richard the elephant groom who admitted he would rather spend Christmas with his "ele's" than with his family! Christmas was a peaceful day, one which meant the animals had nothing else to do but eat, sleep and relax. I remembered the previous Christmas season when with Gandey's Circus, the veteran clown Alex Halls had sat up late on Christmas Eve and wrapped up individual custard cream biscuits for the animals. Each had his or her name beautifully inscribed on a little tag. Being a sentimentalist I too had provided the animals with a Christmas gift in the shape of some tasty titbit, but I did not go to the trouble of wrapping them up, except of course for the 'Kids'. It gave me much pleasure to play Santa and deliver exotic fruits and cake to the elephants, camels, Sahara and horses. Harry had some Christmas cake, and the lions tigers and Ikon the leopard had a mouthful of turkey breast.

To most circus artistes the caravans in which they live are their only homes. Some do purchase houses to which they travel to on holidays or in periods in which they are out of work. Most prefer their caravans, so subsequently the majority of the Circus World artistes stayed in their mobile homes for Christmas Day at Cardiff, enjoying the free time available. Some of us had clubbed together and provided ourselves with a Christmas dinner complete with turkey, pudding and all the trimmings which we prepared in the Pavilion cafeteria. Any artiste or member of staff who was not being catered for by family came along and someone rigged up a portable television, as watching the 'box' is a luxury for hard-working circus folk. Fred, Betsy and Anna came along to the celebration and a very festive time was had by all. Fred proved adept at cracker pulling and Anna demonstrated to one and all that the correct way of eating Christmas pudding was to first of all step in it with both feet. The chimps loved social gatherings and would show off unmercifully!

At Cardiff, they donned paper hats, played games and partook of the odd sip or in their case gulp, of wine and beer, especially if they thought I was preoccupied elsewhere. I would have to admit that the most ardent animal liberationalist would be right in commenting that a wild chimp would not behave in such a fashion, and yet I feel it would be Betsy, Fred and Anna's wild counterparts who would be missing out.

After lunch the three animals curled up on chairs and feeling very full, had a long snooze. Betsy sat on my lap and did keep awake for the Queen's speech, well after all, having performed for Royalty it was the least one could do.

Boxing Day was an end to festivities for the circus folk in more ways than one. The circus was giving three shows and all had been heavily booked far in advance so we were expecting three sell-outs.

The day dawned to another rain storm. I hurried from the building where I had given the chimps breakfast, to the stables where the other animals were being seen to. I grabbed a pitchfork and gave a hand with the mucking out. It might have been wet and cold outside but inside it was warm thanks to the straw and body heat of the animals. In no time I had removed my coat and sweater. As we worked we listened to the radio which was situated on the very top of the pile of straw bales at one end of the tent. It was on at full volume to overcome the sound of the animals munching away and the noise of the rain pelting against the canvas roof. The radio had already been moved twice before resting on its present position. At first it had been an easy target for Sahara's tongue which had resulted in several changes of volume and station. It was then moved to a wheelbarrow, not far from the camel pen, where it had almost been vandalised by an inquisitive Joey, who had abandoned his usual viewpoint between the camel's humps in order to investigate the music box. Now, safely out of everyone's reach it was emitting the usual Christmas music, old favourites such as 'Jingle Bells' and inappropriately, considering the weather, 'White Christmas'. The announcer on the radio gave out flood warnings to residents living in small towns and villages surrounding Cardiff and all of us in the stable listened in disbelief. Someone remarked how sad it was to have a Christmas ruined by flood, and how lucky we were not to be out there.

Just then, Margaret popped her head through the stable door, and asked if any of us had looked at the river recently? We all shook our heads and put on our coats and followed her out of the stable to view the water. The sight that greeted us was indeed a surprise, the water was alarmingly high. At various points along the river bank council workmen were busy building walls of sandbags, watched by policemen. One of them spotted the small group of circus folk and came along to reassure us that all was well, and to say he did not expect the water level to increase any further. His confidence was not shared by one of the local youngsters, who plagued the circus each day hoping to help out with the animals, and who remarked that a high tide was due shortly, and then the river was bound to swell further.

The company prepared for the first performance under a potential threat of flooding, which was not the best of situations in which to perform. Everyone tried to forget about the river as the music started in the hall and they donned their make-up. The audience arrived and consisted largely of families with children looking forward to a Christmas treat. The Pavilion was indeed going to be packed. The artistes made their way to the building and gazed anxiously towards the river which did not in fact look as if it had risen any further during the last half hour or so.

Water was apparently sweeping down from the hill and valley streams which could hardly cope with the volume of water caused by so much recent rain. As the overture commenced a rumour was circulating that further down the river there was flooding and sandbags had not been able to hold the water back. There was even talk of cancelling the performance. The show had started and the mixed wild animal act was drawing big applause from the audience. I assisted with dismantling the ring cage and as the zebras and spotted ponies trotted into the ring I went to get the 'Kids' ready for the show.

Sensing I was nervous and ill at ease the chimps did not give one of their better performances. As I led them back to their quarters I apologised to them in case I had worried them, and I spent a few more moments with them talking in a reassuring tone. I left the chimps with some fruit and hurried back to resume my duties in the ring.

Just before the interval a police car pulled up outside the Pavilion and two uniformed officers rushed up to the box office and informed Carol Gardner, our chief clerk, that the building would have to be evacuated immediately as flooding was imminent. Apparently the river had burst its banks a little upstream and because of the position of the Pavilion in a basin below the river, the police were worried that we were in danger.

It was hard to have to cancel what was going to be the best day of the season, but of course the safety of the public was first and foremost. The audience was reluctant to leave, as like many of the circus folk, they doubted the possibility of a flood in what was practically the centre of Cardiff. However after they realised the show was going to stop they began to evacuate. A large majority headed for the box office to demand a refund, and an exasperated Carol and box office staff did their best to cope, police urging managed to persuade them that they must leave, and leave now with refunds to be obtained at a later date. One or two customers were not entirely satisfied with that, and amazingly there were still people at the box office when the first water began to appear at the doors of the building.

The bank of the river by the building itself held firm, but further up in the park, near a sports centre the river had spilled over and it was from this direction the water came. Before the water's arrival and as the public were filing out, the artistes and staff sat around wondering what to do. Most of us felt that it was just a precaution, perhaps due to the nearness of high tide and by the evening the alarm would be over and we could resume performances. Just then a shout came from the direction of the stables that water was indeed appearing and we rushed outside, most of us still in costume.

It is an incredible feeling to see water appearing as if from nowhere, and the speed with which it was deepening was alarming. Even so, none of us believed, even then that the water would get too deep. Within minutes the water was at least two feet deep and rising.

Back at the box office Carol delivered a few meaningful phrases to the last few punters haggling over money and convinced them they should get into cars and flee. Carol and the rest of the staff in true loyalty gathered up the remaining money and tickets together with other office equipment and took them to safety without a thought for personal belongings. Likewise the animal staff headed by Margaret made the animals their first concern.

Everything was happening quickly and water was rising, anyone who had doubted the flood, was now persuaded of the river's intentions. The animals were led into the building at first, as by now the stables were thoroughly waterlogged.

Artistes not helping with the animals now attempted to hitch up their caravans and pull away. Jimmy Chipperfield had managed to get his big American trailer off the site and pulled it onto a bridge overlooking the park making it the H.Q. for everyone. Some of the artistes and staff also managed to get their vehicles and caravans away and drove off, not knowing where they were heading and anxiously leaving behind members of the family to cope with the animals, not knowing what would happen to them. Driving around the streets was chaos as many roads had been blocked because of flooding, but eventually the caravans were invited to stay at a sports centre car park on the outskirts of Cardiff. Closer inspection of the vehicles at a later date revealed a lot of damage, such was the rush to get away none of the trailers were prepared, and subsequently electric cables had been ripped off and everything inside had been jostled to such an extent that much had been smashed. Yet these were the lucky ones, so many of the mobile homes had not been able to be pulled clear and were now at the mercy of the waters.

Sahara the giraffe, ran into his travelling wagon without any fuss and was towed to higher ground under the supervision of Mr. Larenty the father of tightwire artiste Brenda. Sahara normally played a game with anyone attempting to load him, waiting until he was bribed with a sweet or similar, but he must have realised the emergency of the occasion as he sped into his wagon as quickly as his long legs could carry him.

Water was now seeping into the hall itself and Margaret was valiantly organising help to lead animals from the building, with anyone spare being roped in to give assistance. Brenda Larenty herself, still in costume but with Wellington boots on her feet and a raincoat thrown over her shoulders was coping marvellously with three liberty horses who were nervously skittish. The animals were led out of the hall and into the city where they just kept on walking in the hope of eventually finding somewhere in the city to install the animals for the night.

This exodus of strange creatures was not without incident. Many animals broke loose and ran off much to everyone's alarm. Jock the Highland Bull and Peter the Yak broke away from the convoy and disappeared from view.

Several camels ran off and were later caught at the railway station, jokes that they were trying to book one way tickets to a station in Mongolia were not appreciated. Joy Sloan had her life saved by a runaway zebra. She had been wading along through the deepening water when her foot went into an open drain, down she went, but was saved by the fact that she was able to reach out for a passing zebra and was pulled clear!

Whilst the animals were being led out of the hall, I enlisted the help of the ring staff in getting the chimps clear of danger. I had the boys drag the heavy wooden sleeping dens up the stairs from the room in which the chimps had been living. Piling the dens with straw I installed the hooting and excited chimps inside. The dens were difficult to manhandle and this was further complicated by the fact that to get the chimp dens onto the stairs from their room, we had to go via a trap door as the other exits were now blocked by water. We never did get Joey's den out before water came into the room, and I had luckily taken him out earlier on collar and lead and tethered him to a section of tiered seating in the hall itself.

I could not believe my eyes as I saw the room in which a few hours earlier the chimps had played, now begin to fill with water. The three chimp dens were positioned on the much higher stage and I surrounded them with bales of straw that had been stored there.

All the rooms below stairs including most of the dressing rooms were now flooded. Some of the staff made valiant efforts to retrieve costumes and props which were piled onto the stage. Eventually they were beaten back. The main floor of the building was under about six inches of water, but satisfied that Joey and the chimps were safe in their high positions on the stage I went outside to see if I was needed elsewhere.

Back in the stables all except the elephants had been evacuated. Roger Cawley and Carl Fischer Jnr were unshackling the elephant tethers, reaching underwater to do so. The elephants themselves amazingly, were having a whale of a time, trumpeting with the delight of having an unexpected bath and were squirting water everywhere including over Carl and Roger!

The elephants were led by Carl through the water and out into the city. Where was Carl to take them however? Five playful elephants were one thing, but Carl knew that playfulness could lead to panic if the elephants took fright, and the thought of rampaging elephants through the centre of Cardiff was a nightmare. So, Carl keeping calm ordered the animals into file and with groom Richard he led them through the city. They kept on walking until coming to a farm where the kindly farmer installed the unexpected guests in a barn!

The site of the Pavilion and park varies greatly, dipping and sloping. In some areas the thick murky water was now almost waist deep and was beginning to reach inside the caravans that had not been pulled clear. I passed Margaret Chipperfield's brand new American trailer, which was awash with black river water. I take my hat off to Margaret in her handling of the crisis. No one could have worked harder to ensure the animals were not harmed in the flood.

I could see her heading the motley crew of animals and assorted staff as they headed for somewhere warm and dry. The local people were very helpful indeed. Lady shoppers who previously had been holding bags of shopping suddenly found themselves temporary minders of assorted camels and llamas. One such lady was given Johnny the Shetland pony and a circus dog to mind for a few moments. However she promptly marched them off home and after drying them and giving them something to eat she made them comfortable — in her kitchen! It was there that they stayed until the water subsided and they could return to the circus. The lady was quite undisturbed by the two animals in her kitchen — in fact she was sorry to see them go!

As Margaret disappeared I turned a corner and came across the wild animal trailer, and to my horror I realised that I had been so preoccupied with seeing Sahara off and with making sure the chimps were safe, that I had not given much thought to what was happening to the lions, tigers, leopard and bear. Because of the tight parking at Cardiff the huge trailer had been positioned against the back of the Pavilion. The tractor unit had unhitched and had returned to the circus farm, so subsequently there had been nothing to pull the trailer free. Joy Sloan had apparently asked for help from any truck drivers in the area via the CB radio and several drivers tried to reach the circus site, but were prevented by the flood.

Roger Cawley, soaked through, was sitting on a part of the trailer, checking if the animals were OK — he enquired after the chimps and told me to go and get dry. I then realised I was still in costume, and soaked to the skin.

On the way back to the hall I passed my own caravan, and poked my head inside. The water had seeped in through the door and the floor was under water. I paddled my way to the back of the trailer and stood on the bed, stripped off and from a cupboard above the water line, dug out some dry clothes. As I was changing I looked around at the sodden trailer, which also smelt awful, as sewage from the over flowing drains had mingled in with the river water. For the first time the enormity of what had actually happened hit me, and I felt truly miserable.

I was anxious to head back to the chimps but before I did I rather selfishly bundled together my most precious possessions, tape recorder, files containing passport and other documents, my poetry collection and some photographs. With these I waded out towards the bridge where Jimmy Chipperfield's trailer was still parked, despite being warned of the possible danger to the bridge should the waters continue to rise at their present rate for any length of time. I bundled my goods inside and refusing a coffee headed back to the chimps.

Wading back through the water I passed Joy Sloan making the last of several trips retrieving office equipment. Joy looked really down and out, but she is a tough lady of old circus stock and in an effort to smile she jokingly informed me the flood was my fault! I had a habit of singing whilst I was working and Joy was always reprimanding me for doing so, as singing in the Big Top was always considered unlucky according to old circus superstition.

"You're responsible Mr. Hibling!" she quipped. She asked me where I was going and I told her that I naturally must go to the chimps as I had nowhere to take them. She promised to try to sort something out and she headed for some dry ground.

Back inside the hall, the chimps were pleased to see me. I had not been gone too long but they were a little frightened. I sat with them and talked reassuringly to them. In a relatively short time the water in the hall was waist deep, though still a long way off from reaching the edge of the stage.

I gazed down into the water and laughed as I saw the circus' pelican and the duck from Tommy Fossett's clown act swimming merrily in the water, having come into the building literally on the crest of a wave and they were now having the time of their lives.

A thought occurred to me that I ought to wade across the hall and reach the public telephones in the foyer, where I could ring my parents in Sussex, just in case they had heard of the flood and were worried. I jumped off the stage and made my way into the foyer. Getting through the doors from the main hall into the foyer was extremely difficult due to water pressure on both sides, but I eventually managed it and reached the 'phone. I had no money on me but I could transfer charges I thought. I picked up the 'phone and to my relief I heard the dialling tone. However just as I began to dial 100 for the operator the line went dead. I truly felt wretched.

Struggling back into the hall was as difficult as struggling out, but I got through and made my way back to the chimps. I passed Joey sitting on his section of seating, made sure he was not cold, tickled his ear and told him what a good boy he was. I reached the chimps, and being wet once more I opened one of the hampers that were stored on the stage and changed into a costume, a clown's baggy suit. Feeling miserable, but looking an idiot, I sat with the chimps and wondered just what the next move would be. I knew that Roger was sitting outside with the wild animals, Carl was somewhere with the elephants, and Margaret and her grooms were somewhere else with whatever stock they still had hold of.

I hoped Joy was trying to find somewhere for the chimps to go — but where? Three chimps and a baboon are not the easiest of animals to house, so perhaps it was best to stay where we were, at least they were warm and dry upon the stage. Surely, somebody would bring food out to us if the flood lasted any length of time? As I was contemplating all this I suddenly heard a very ominous creaking sound. I realised that the water in the hall was dislodging the metal supports holding up the circus seating, to which Joey was tethered! I feared it might collapse and drown the baboon, so I jumped into the water again in order to bring him back to the stage.

Some of the floorboards had come up with the water so subsequently the water was deeper in places than I imagined, and on my first leap onto the hall floor I went straight under. I regained my footing and made my way to Joey. I reached him and wondered how he would react to plunging into the water — this would be a test of his respect for me.

He clung tight to my neck and bravely followed me into the water. It must have been alarming for him, but his trust in me was evidently greater than his fear of what was going on around him. At one point he had to swim when I again lost my footing, but at no time did he attempt to pull away, panic or bite me. I was very proud of him. We reached the stage and I tethered him to the large iron staircase that went from the stage to the theatre flies. I broke open one of the straw bales that I had piled around the chimp dens in order to dry him off and keep him warm. After a search I came across some apples and bananas which I distributed among them. Now that I was with them the chimps were calm and sat quietly peering out of the dens towards the hall.

It was now getting dark and they began to rearrange the straw inside their dens and settle down to sleep. I opened the door of Anna's den to give her a quick cuddle and to make sure her straw was arranged in a fashion which would make her comfortable and sleep. I then went back to the hamper and for the umpteenth time that afternoon changed my wet clothes.

Just then, a torch flashed, cutting through the darkness at the side of the stage and we were joined by a ringboy, whose name I am ashamed to admit, now escapes me. He told me that the water was getting deeper outside, although he had reached the building fairly easily but he was wet through.

Apparently the artistes, staff, and local householders, who had been flooded had congregated at Cardiff's largest hotel where soup had been handed out. Jimmy Chipperfield and David Balding had made a quick count of numbers and all except Brenda and myself could be accounted for. Brenda's parents were becoming frantic, but the young tightwire artiste, after walking miles to get the horses to safety was making her way back to the city, and had got lost — and was not drowned as everyone had feared.

It was guessed that I would be with the chimps still, and the lad had come to see for himself. So there we sat, two lads, three chimps and a baboon, oh, and not forgetting the pelican and the duck.

The water level had risen, but was remaining constant when suddenly one of the swing doors leading to an exit burst open due to outside pressure, and a wave of water burst through. The influx of water did not raise the inside level at all, but what with the darkness, the eerie atmosphere of the deserted hall, and the water coming through the doors I must admit I felt a little panicky.

We both realised that in our heart of hearts we knew that it was impossible to disappear under water in a building the size of the Sophia Gardens Pavilion, but even so, we decided to get the chimps out of their dens. Wrapping them in spare costumes and horse blankets we climbed the metal staircase into the flies. I think we were overreacting a bit, and Fred, roused from sleep, probably thought so too, but there we were, sat high up in the roof of the building. The flies consist of narrow metal walkways from which tabs (curtains) and scenery are 'flown' into position. As we made ourselves comfortable at such great height, I learnt more of what the flood had done to the community.

Apparently most of the city surrounding the Sophia Gardens had been affected to some degree by the flooding. In the valleys the damage had been greater and it was feared some people might have drowned. One of our own circus staff, Ron Allen had nearly met a watery end when he realised that his pet dog was still in his caravan and had waded back to rescue him. The two of them had been swept along by a sudden heavy current and Ron had saved them both by clinging on to a lamp-post where he was rescued by a police boat.

As we sat and talked we wondered if anyone *was* concerned about us! We decided to send an S.O.S. signal with the aid of a torch which we could shine through a skylight in the roof. As time went by I was amused to reflect that the whole saga was beginning to sound like an Enid Blyton adventure novel for children, with Joey, the 'Kids' and myself becoming the 'Famous Five'.

I started to dream up book titles; "Famous Five and the Great Circus Flood!", or "Famous Five and the River of Fear" or even "Famous Five Underwater". My train of thought was interrupted by a shout via a loudhailer. David Balding was speaking to us from a dry point near the bridge. He told us to sit tight and we would be rescued shortly.

Sure enough, within half an hour a speedboat was launched by the police. We climbed down from the flies and opened a door that led from the back of the stage to the outside. The water was lapping the edge so the boat was able to pull right alongside and we all climbed in. I decided for safety sake I should leave Joey where he was. I was informed that the water had not risen in the last half hour and was expected to fall if anything. To make sure, I took Joey a little further up the staircase to within reach of his straw bed. I was not too sure where I was going with the chimps, but I knew I could handle them for as long as it took to get things back to normal. I did not know for how long I could control Joey in the centre of the city. He was safe where he was I felt, and luckily David in the boat had brought along some fruit for him. Although I was not entirely happy about leaving him, it did seem to be for the best.

We sped over the water and I reflected that only yesterday I had walked down the streets which now were under water, with the roofs of cars only just visible. I suddenly exclaimed to David, "What is happening to the lions, tigers and Harry?" David explained that alarmingly, the water had crept into their cages but they were able to keep themselves above water. Carl was alongside them in a boat, having left the elephants in the charge of groom Richard at the farm where they were being stabled temporarily. It was a terrifying situation and Carl was to stay with the animals all the time the area was flooded.

I hugged Anna closely, and whispered a quick prayer for the wild animals, hoping the waters would subside quickly. Anna buried her head into my chest while Fred and Betsy hooted apprehensively beneath their blankets. It did not take us long to reach dry land and we were greeted by Jimmy Chipperfield, anxious to get us into the nearest warm building. We all accepted gratefully, mugs of warm sweet tea. I was so preoccupied in getting the chimps dry and settled, that it took a few seconds to realise where we were. It turned out to be a funeral parlour, the nearest place which was dry and warm! I began to envisage newspaper headlines the following morning, "Chimps run amok in undertakers!" not that Fred, Betsy or Anna were in a mood to run amok anywhere.

They kept close to me and looked very tired. It was imperative that we found somewhere suitable for them to spend the night and David Balding had set about finding us somewhere to go.

A 'phone call to the RSPCA proved fruitless, and the nearest zoo, which would have meant a long drive anyway, had no suitable cages spare. I was beginning to get very concerned, as the chimps were getting tired and irritable.

One of the policemen helping out with flood relief suggested that we might be able to install the chimps in the local police station — in the cells!

After ringing around he found a police station near the docks that had empty cells. The chimps and I sped off in a police car ready to be 'detained at Her Majesty's pleasure'. We were now so exhausted we would have been happy to be detained at anyone's pleasure. . .

It was very late when the three chimpanzees and a bedraggled, costumed trainer arrived at the police station. The officers at the station fetched some food and drink for us all, a change of clothing and very shortly the chimps were fast asleep in the comfortable police cells. Anna was tucked up in a cat basket that one of the officers had found. I slept on a bench outside the cells, grateful to be warm and dry.

During the night a drunk had been brought into the station to 'cool off' after some disorderly behaviour in the city centre. The 'Kids' and I were so tired that we slept through all the noise. The police, not wanting to disturb us, locked the drunk inside a broom cupboard where he sobered up, not before complaining loudly at the size of police cells!

Back at the Sophia Gardens, daylight showed a very sorry scene, with the caravans that had not been pulled clear now waterlogged. Many of them, thanks to the force of the tide, having been swept from their original parking places. An MG sports car belonging to Graham Webster of the publicity team, was completely submerged and half a tree trunk swept down with the flood waters had smashed through the windscreen. Jock the Highland bull and Peter, the

Chimp assures the Author 'it's alright'. *(Author's collection)*

Himalayan yak, who had pulled away from the convoy of fleeing animals were found to be safe, although marooned on a small patch of high parkland.

Carl Fischer was still with the wild animals, who tragically had to spend the flood standing with their heads held high above the water level. Amazingly, after the flood was over and many of the artistes and animals had colds and chills to contend with, neither Harry, the leopard or the tigers or lions showed any ill-effect from their ordeal.

Back at the police station Betsy had discovered that her 'long arm', when stretched through the bars of her cell could reach a switch and turn off all the lights in the police station. This caused quite a stir until the cause of sudden darkness had been found! The officers at the station were highly amused to think that they were playing hosts to three highly unusual guests and spoilt them something rotten. Toys, fruit and sweets were brought in for them daily. The chimps had a constant stream of visitors, and the press had a field day. Fred, our photogenic star, was photographed wearing police helmets, doing a spot of typing in the office, and answering the 'phone. Even the national press paid us a visit, and a film sequence showing the chimps in their temporary quarters ended an edition of ITV's News At Ten. This finished with a delightful shot of Anna disappearing into her basket, then returning to peer over the top as if to say 'Goodnight' — and also to fool everyone into thinking she was angelic!

After a couple of days the waters had subsided enough for us all to return to the site, and we said goodbye to our police hosts. Chimps being chimps the cells were not exactly spotless and I apologised for the mess. I did return to give a hand with cleaning them later, which was the least I could do, but the police said not to worry, as the more usual inmates often left them in far worse a condition — the mind boggles.

I expect the police at Cardiff have not forgotten their chimp guests, and that many jokes and stories have been told about them, but neither shall I forget all the kindness and concern that the officers showed us during our misfortune.

The main objective now, was to get the circus back to normal and to reopen. Joey was non-committal in his greeting, the flood apparently had not unduly upset him. Well, he took everything in his stride. Various people, amongst them Carl and Roger had kept an eye on him making sure he was fed and provided with warm bedding at night.

The flood had left everything covered with thick black slime. A big clean-up operation was undertaken, a mammoth task made all the more difficult as there was nowhere clean to put anything down to begin with. My first job was to make sure the chimp quarters were clean and dry, and afterwards I set about retrieving the chimp props and clean them off, as well as giving a hand wherever I was needed.

All the caravans that had been left behind were in an awful state and artistes and staff began to assess the damage and to retrieve whatever they could. The Chipperfields hired brand new caravans to give artistes and staff a temporary roof over their heads, the dry cleaners and local launderettes did a roaring trade as costumes and everyday clothes were cleaned. Everybody, artistes and management included, got stuck in and set about cleaning the hall and restoring the glitter to enable the show to reopen.

Margaret and staff restored the stables to order and all the animals returned from the various farms where they had been stabled. Jock and Peter turned up, no doubt motivated by their stomachs! Reluctantly, Johnny the Shetland and the little circus dog were returned by the kindly lady who had given them bed and breakfast in her kitchen home. All the Cardiff people had been very kind, and gifts of clothing were sent to the circus for us. The Council set up a fund for all people who had been affected by the flooding.

Local support was evident when the circus re-opened within a few days, and we were able to display one or two 'Full House' signs during the remaining few weeks of the season.

My own caravan was a 'write-off' and was never to be inhabited again. I had also lost my contact lenses in the flood, and being too vain to wear spectacles in the ring, whilst awaiting new lenses I was forced to work with everything appearing blurred, such is my vision without lenses. I would remove my glasses upon entering the ring, leaving it up to the chimps to virtually guide me through the act. Carl Fischer was prompted to remark that he thought the act was better with the chimps in charge.

It was whilst looking for my lenses, and trying to see if there was anything else in my caravan worth retrieving that I came across a soggy unopened Christmas present from my brother and sister-in-law. I opened it and let out a loud laugh, it was a cassette with recordings by my favourite classical composer Handel — selections from his "Water Music!"

Yet that was not the only ironic ending to the flood saga. The poor old Pavilion that had struggled bravely through the flooding was to suffer further, and this time fatal indignities a couple of winters later. Heavy snowfall in the Welsh capital caused the building's roof to collapse and eventually she was demolished and stands no more. A very sad ending for a fine place of entertainment.

Happily, circuses still feature in Cardiff's Christmas festivities and at the time of writing I read in the circus trade paper World's Fair that the Circus Hoffman is to play a winter season under a Big Top, on the old Pavilion site.

Chapter 5

Tea-party magic & three 'live' bears

Mary Chipperfield had kept in touch with the flood-stricken circus via the telephone, ringing each day from the winter circus at Manchester. When the two seasons finished we all met up again at the Farm and a lot of stories were told over coffee about the adventures that had befallen the animals and staff.

My bedraggled caravan had been towed to the Farm from Cardiff by my Uncle John, who had been a great help to me. He had rushed down from his Wiltshire home to the circus in order to see if he could give any assistance. I took a few days leave from the Winter Quarters to purchase a new trailer, which in due course was inspected by the chimps and given their approval.

Within a few weeks the flood was all but forgotten and life settled back to normal, well as normal as is possible at the Farm. Jimmy Chipperfield's Circus World was to make another tour and new acts had to be rehearsed for the 1980 season. Margaret was following her elder sister to the Blackpool Tower Circus where she would be presenting a novel grouping of two African elephants, two zebras and two Shetland ponies. It was Mary therefore who would be touring with Circus World and headlining the programme when it returned to the Yarmouth Hippodrome later on in the summer. She was going to ride High School, present the Big and Little number, plus a new routine for the Arab Horses and Indian, the skewbald stallion that Margaret had shown at Cardiff.

As well as the horses Mary would be rehearsing a new mixed wild animal act that would debut at Yarmouth. On tour, the cage act was Mary's tigers presented either by herself or Carl Fischer Jnr. He had returned to present the elephants and also some young Canadian black bears, as well as the exotics; the giraffe, camels and cattle.

I was to work on a new routine with the chimps which would star Anna, Joey now having been retired. I was also given a new role for the tenting tour, that of Ringmaster. As already explained a Ringmaster's job is a difficult and demanding one, but it is made even more so when you are also presenting animals in the show that you are acting as Ringmaster for. This also meant some very quick costume changes and at one point introducing myself.

The winter and the following spring saw the chimps learning new tricks for their act. Betsy had perfected a somersault which had taken most of the previous summer to teach. I began by holding Betsy's hand and jumping up and down with her. Being a springy sort of animal it was an easy step to turn her head over heels as she jumped

Jimmy Chipperfield's 1980 Circus World Tour. *(David Jamieson)*

Mary Chipperfield riding Pedro, her High School Stallion. *(David Jamieson)*

and a somersault was born. All that was required was time to encourage her to perform the feat unaided. Fred and Betsy also learned to do some very fast roll-overs, holding onto each other's hands and feet, but Fred stole the show with his mastering of stilt walking. Fred had grasped the idea very quickly and enjoyed stomping around on them.

An interesting postscript to this trick was a twist in the routine that the chimps put in entirely by themselves. One performance Fred was near to finishing his stilt walking spot and was returning to the seats when Betsy suddenly reached out in an unusual ad lib and pulled one of the stilts from underneath Fred, much to his and everyone elses' surprise. Down he went looking very crest fallen. The strange thing was that in the next performance Fred tempted Betsy to do the same thing again, and the two of them repeated the routine every night. It always brought forth a big laugh from the audience, although to me it was never as funny as when it happened the first time as then the look on Fred's face was so comical as he toppled off his stilts.

Anna entered the act with gusto. Her obvious 'baby' appeal meant she had to do little in the ring except to be herself and as such would always win an audience's heart. She had mastered her ABC learning to stay put on her seat until she was called for although as her confidence grew so did her cheek. As she was never on a leash she would often leave her seat when my back was turned and creep up on me from behind in a variety of poses. As soon as I spun round she would rush to her feet and return as quickly as possible to her seat, only to resume her 'stalking' of me when I had my back to her again. She also developed a tendency for stripping! Every so often, whenever the mood took her, she would suddenly rush into the middle of the ring and rip off all her clothes! The first occasion that it happened it was so funny, that for a few minutes I and the entire ring staff were helpless with laughter.

Anna took over Joey's role of manipulating the seesaw for Fred and Betsy, but her real success was in her parodies of the older chimps' tricks. For instance, Fred would perform a very fast series of roll-overs after which Anna would very slowly and deliberately perform her version of a roll-over accompanied by a loud drum roll. Later in the season she even managed to emulate Betsy's tightwire routine, albeit with assistance from me. Her efforts were always amusing, particularly as she would rush to me as soon as the older animals had completed their routine, as if to say eagerly "My turn now!"

Her favourite trick however, was the swing routine in which she would sit in a swing and Fred would push her. After some patient training the trick was very funny. I taught Anna to run back to the swing every time she was removed as if to say "More please". This would be followed by me removing her, only to see Fred leap into the swing for his turn. This would usually end up with the swing toppling

Fred on stilts. *(Author's collection)*

over and all of us ending up in a heap on the floor! Yes, after Anna joined the act it was never the same again.

For the 1980 tour a brand new white and red Big Top was purchased from Italy, and new groups of speciality acts had joined the show. For the first few weeks the very talented Spanish Garcia troupe joined us. The troupe consisted of father, mother, two sons and five attractive daughters. Between them they performed an amazing variety of acts; solo trapeze, foot juggling, hair hanging, and perch. All the family combined to present a rousing 'Russian swing' number. Later, when they departed to Ireland, the South African Flying Cherokees joined us, presenting a flying trapeze act with Annie, the lady from the troupe performing her 'corde-lisse' routine. This is a sort of aerial ballet on a hanging rope.

Barry Lappy, a teenage trick cyclist who was also booked, having recently appeared as a featured artiste with the mighty three ring Ringling Bros, Barnum and Bailey Circus in America. Barry was a superb cyclist although I personally felt he lacked warmth in the ring. He was assisted in the ring by his elderly parents, who approached me within days of appearing on the show and said to me, "Mr Hibling, as you kow Barry will be following your act and working on the same boards, and you realise that should they make a mess on the boards it will be very difficult for our son to work." I did my best to assure them that such an accident would not occur and that the animals

Baby Anna with author in the ring. (Geoff Stevens)

wore nappies. I did omit to inform them of Anna's infamous stripteases though. Later, when the show went into Yarmouth the programme was changed and I followed Barry into the ring. I had to fight hard to stop myself from stating that if Barry messed on the boards, it would be very difficult for the chimps to work!

Our clowns for the 1980 tour were two Mexican brothers, the Martinez. They were subtle clowns, with little make-up and their routines incorporated much mime. It was very interesting to see them adapt and change their act to suit English humour, and at the intimate Yarmouth buildings, so good to circus clowns, they were a big hit.

In 1980 we were joined by a young German lad who was to be apprentice trainer to Mary. Thorsten Khormann was his name, and the son of a respected animal trainer who felt his son would benefit from the experience of working with the Chipperfields. Thorsten is a very likeable person, but he somehow had the unfortunate gift of being able to get on the wrong side of Mary and upset her.

Time after time he would incur Mary's wrath (not a pleasant sight!) by forgetting to do certain tasks, or foolishly doing things "his way". Frequently, throughout each day at the Farm, and on the circus, we would hear Mary shout "THORSTEN!", and we knew the lad was in trouble — again.

In between getting shouted at he did manage to learn the art of animal training from Mary. He has since had great success with two animal acts into which he has injected his individual personality and made his own. The first was a hilarious 'Farmyard revue' which featured a dog, chicken, donkey, goats and two wonderful pigs. Thorsten adopted the style of country yokel when he presented the act, complete with Wellington boots, and straw in the mouth. Later he presented a group of sealions for the Chipperfields, with which he is still working.

Thorsten Khormann successfully presenting Mary Chipperfields sealions. (David Jamieson)

I hope Thorsten does not suffer the same fate as I did when working with the Brighton sealions. One afternoon in their eagerness to obtain the fish with which I was feeding them I happened to get bitten by one of the troupe. The bite in my hand was quite severe and required stitches and I was taken to Brighton's General hospital. This was where the problems started. I was ushered into a room and was soon administered to by a doctor who was of Oriental birth, and who turned out had no idea of what a sealion was. This proved to be quite hysterical and I soon forget about the pain as I tried to explain to a bemused doctor just what a sealion was. Alas, he never did discover what had bitten me, and at one stage he came to the conclusion it was some sort of bumble bee. Then, thanks to my vocal imitation of a sealion he decided it was a dog, finally we both settled on the fact that it was a fish with nasty teeth!

I sometimes think that I am accident prone for on another occasion on the 1980 tour I fell on to an up-turned pitchfork, which someone had foolishly left lying about. The spike went right through my knee. On this occasion the hilarities did not occur at the hospital but back at the circus where for the first time (and hopefully the last), I missed a performance. Mary had to present the chimps but had no idea of the new order of tricks and spent most of the act passing the bandstand and through her smile, asking Bandleader George Jones "What comes next?"

For that tour we discarded the Western theme for the chimp act and adopted a style that was to be popular with audiences ever since. All the chimps and myself dressed in identical dungarees and T-shirts. We looked very colourful in the ring, but as I was sporting a beard at the time, it did prompt one of the ring staff to note that it would be very difficult to tell me apart from the chimps!

The new routine for the act was as follows: We would all enter the ring and make a quick circuit with the chimps forming a chain, hands on each other's shoulders. Then to our seats situated in the ring entrance, before Betsy jumped three hurdles after which Anna stole Betsy's applause by running underneath the hurdles with me in hot pursuit.

Fred would perform some very fast roll-overs returning to his seat on the infamous scooter. Anna would mimic the roll-overs before Betsy would manipulate a large globe up and down a seesaw, ending with a one-leg balance on the globe. The globe discarded, the chimps would sit on the seesaw, Fred and Betsy, either end with Anna running up and down in between. This was followed by the swing routine, then Betsy would show off her somersaults and her expertise at walking on her hands. Fred's big solo spot was his stilt walking, and this in turn was followed by Betsy's tightwire routine which included a kneel, a one leg stand and a leap from the platform to my arms. Anna's mimic of this ended with me asking her to leap into my arms

T shirts and dungarees. Anna, Betsy, Fred on the see saw. *(Courtesy Ivan Gould)*

Author and the three chimps take their bow. *(Courtesy Ivan Gould)*

as Betsy had done, only I would deliberately stand too far away from her. She would then climb down the prop and run to me instead, always earning big applause.

The Western whip cracking was retained as it was such a good finale to the act. I would then pick up all the chimps, Fred and Betsy in my arms and little Anna on my shoulders, and make our exit. The act normally lasted six or seven minutes, but if the chimps were in a good mood, and especially if Anna was feeling particularly troublesome, we would last a little longer. Once at Yarmouth during a matinée we stayed on for twelve minutes, and earned a reprimand from the Ringmaster.

Music was an important part of the act and for the second tour of Circus World, we had as Bandleader, the excellent George Jones. George and his wife Gwen are amongst the nicest people I know, George is a gifted musician and has a perfect understanding of circus music, knowing it must compliment but never compete with the artistes in the ring. Circus musicians must also pay close attention to what is going on in the ring, to be ready at a second to change tunes, stop, start at a moment's notice in order to be in harmony with an artiste or animal. The band always follows the act, never the other way round.

George Jones is a quiet unassuming man but with a lovely sense of humour, and throughout the season never once seemed unhappy or moody. He would watch the acts very closely and continually come up with a suggestion for a new tune to suit a certain trick. With the chimps he devised music that was so fitting to the individual tricks that in seven minutes there was no less than thirteen changes of music. Amongst some of the tunes played were, 'The Muppet theme' as the opening music, 'Tweedle Dee and Tweedle Dum', 'Walking my baby back home', 'Capt. Beaky' (for Anna) and 'So what's new' — my own suggestion as it was a personal favourite of mine. George was also very quick with musical ad libs, should anything go wrong in performance. Once when my tightwire prop collapsed he struck up with 'Steptoe & Son'! On another occasion, when wearing new yellow costumes he had the band play songs with 'yellow' in the title for the entire act and we performed to such tunes as 'Yellow River', 'Yellow Bird' and even the Beatles' 'Yellow Submarine'.

Once, as a joke on actor Robin Askwith (of 'Confessions of a Window Cleaner' fame) who was attending a matinée performance, I entered the ring carrying a ladder, and the chimps with sponges and buckets. George immediately struck up the old George Formby hit 'When I'm cleaning windows'.

The tour happily repeated the success of the previous year, and we adopted a similar schedule, playing towns in the Southern Midlands, the South East and the outskirts of London, before heading for a second season at the Yarmouth Hippodrome.

Joy Sloan returned as Front of House Manager, running the concessions and box office in her usual efficient way. I have never known Joy to be ill, except on one occasion at Northampton when she caught a 'bug' which had also affected many of the circus personnel. Subsequently, the show became something of a one-man band, with an unsuspecting public coming face to face with the same people. In the box office selling tickets were Anne Fischer and Mary Chipperfield, with myself inspecting the tickets at the entrance of the Big Top. Showing people to their seats was Carl Fischer. As soon as the performance began, it was myself as Ringmaster that the public saw first, followed by the man who had shown them to their seats and then the lady who had sold them the tickets! It was this same lady, and the Ringmaster that sold ice-cream in the interval.

This tour gave the chimps one of their biggest successes, with an appearance on the celebrated Paul Daniel's Magic Show at the BBC, and the first animal act to do so. John Fisher, the producer of the magic show and a great champion of circus, went down to Gloucester to see the show, and to outline the routine which it was hoped the chimps would perform on the programme as part of a magic sequence with Paul himself. A contract was signed, and which we were to learn later was to provide the great magician himself with much mirth. It stipulated that the chimps were to have guaranteed rest periods whilst filming — as Paul remarked in a later newspaper interview, even he was not granted such luxury!

John explained that it was hoped the chimps would sit at a table with Paul and have a tea-party, during which Paul would attempt to perform a card trick enlisting the aid of the animals. It was decided that we would use the two older chimps and within a few weeks Mary and I were in a Landrover driving down to the BBC studios in London, leaving a sleepy circus at Leicester. Luckily the TV recording was taking place on a build-up day and Mary and I would not miss any performances. Fred and Betsy had drunk an early morning cup of tea and had settled down in a travelling crate, making themselves comfortable for the journey.

After getting lost in London, driving around Lords cricket ground for what seemed an eternity, we found the studios. As soon as we arrived we were greeted by Paul and John, and shown to our rooms. The four of us were treated so well it was very obvious that everyone connected with the show was excited about the chimps being included in the series.

We installed ourselves in the dressing rooms, the chimps pleased with the opportunity to have a play after the long journey. Dressing rooms were very good playgrounds as far as the chimps were concerned, with taps to turn on and off and on again, wardrobes in which to play hide and seek. Also there was an endless fascination with mirrors, and the chimpanzees that lived in them. After playing, the chimps became tired and settled down for a snooze.

Mary and I went and had something to eat in the BBC canteen before joining Paul in the studio to watch the other acts who were appearing in the show as they rehearsed.

Anyone who has ever spent a day at a TV studios watching a programme being recorded will no doubt have experienced the feeling of wonder that anything gets done. At first glance it seems as if all is chaos with people rushing everywhere, lights and cables in a jungle-like confusion as well as costumes and props coming and going. Yet, everything is remarkably well controlled and fits into a tight time schedule, with the programme producers and director very much in control.

With the Magic Show the rehearsals carry on throughout the day before recording the programme in the evening in front of a 'live', invited audience. It was suggested that it would be better not to rehearse the sequence involving the chimps, as it was thought that by leaving them until the evening recording their reactions would be more spontaneous.

However, in order that the various cameramen and technicians would have some idea of what was planned, a short rehearsal was prepared with myself and Paul's son Martin (now a television presenter himself) standing in for Fred and Betsy. Paul began to perform the magic trick that he had prepared when on a cue from John Fisher (who had bribed us earlier) Martin and I began to do our very best at imitating naughty chimps. Throwing crockery and cutlery around we gave, what I thought, was some very lifelike impressions! Our 'performance' achieved the desired effect and had Paul and the technicians in stitches, but even our over-the-top display was nothing to what the real chimps had up their sleeves!

Eventually the audience arrived and all was ready for the recording to begin. The chimps were not appearing until the end of the show, so Mary and I had time to watch most of the recording before going to get Fred and Betsy ready. The chimps had had a full day, playing and exploring but were still full of life as we dressed them in their smart new dungarees, and yellow T-shirts with their names printed on, which the BBC had specially made for them.

Back in the studio a table had been set, piled high with delightful and tempting treats such as jellies, cakes, fruit, rice-pudding and sweets.

Scattered about on the table were one or two props that it was hoped the chimps would play with. Paul Daniels delivered a quick speech to the audience explaining that he had asked for two special volunteers from the audience to assist him in the final trick of the show. As he spoke we installed the animals at the table which was hidden from the audience by a screen. Paul's speech was interrupted by a loud hoot as the chimps had spotted the food, but as the audience had not seen the chimps nor had they expected to see them, there was huge applause when the screen was lifted and the owners of the hoots were revealed.

Fred and Betsy were in seventh heaven, surrounded by piles of foodstuff normally only received as a treat. They hooted and grunted with delight and almost ignored Paul as he sat between the two animals at the table.

They did not know quite what to eat or drink first and their eagerness amused the audience greatly. The magician attempted to enlist the chimps' attention in his trick but his pleas for assistance were ignored by the two animals whose only thought was food. Paul, a master of ad lib was able to use this to his advantage, and the whole tea-party was fast becoming a hilarious riot.

Fred was eventually persuaded to 'pick a card' from Paul's pack, just as Betsy released a whole load of carnival streamers from a box. Paul's attention momentarily diverted, Fred stuck the card in a bowl of rice-pudding. After "reprimanding" Betsy for fiddling with the props, Paul retrieved the soggy card from the rice-pudding and persuaded Fred to make a mark on the card with a pen. Fred, with a mouthful of cake duly obliged. Fred felt it was time to give his host some thank you kisses, and whilst this was going on Paul gave the card to Betsy to hold. Of course we all knew that Betsy would perform her famous paper ripping trick, thus enabling Paul to express a wonderful look of mock horror.

Having salvaged all but one of the pieces of card he placed them in a handkerchief that he gave Fred to hold. Paul announced that for the next part of the trick he would need a banana and luckily he had one in his pocket. Whilst he was explaining this Betsy delved into his pocket and stole the said banana and began to eat it. None of us had known for certain if Betsy would perform the pickpocketing on cue, but as far as food was concerned she did not miss a trick! Paul's face was a picture as he discovered the theft. Order was restored when he revealed another plastic banana that he had installed as a precaution.

From inside of this one he revealed a small piece of card, and this, unbelievably matched the pieces that Fred had in the handkerchief. At the conclusion of this trick there was thunderous applause from the audience. Fred and Betsy in an unusual display of emotion, hooted and kissed Paul in an expression of congratulations.

The trick was simple and effective, but the whole sequence had been cleverly handled by Paul. My admiration for him increased greatly. He had been in control of the situation all the time, even when it appeared that the chimps were getting the better of him. He did not let the chimps upstage him, but at the same time he did not belittle or ridicule them. That the chimps were having a riotous time was obvious, and the end result was superb television, making a big impression on the public.

The clip 'Paul Daniels and the chimps' has now been repeated on BBC no less than seven times. Quite apart from the original show being repeated a couple of times, the clip has turned up on 'Points of View', on Noel Edmonds 'Multi-coloured swap shop', and when Paul was asked to donate a favourite clip from his series to the BBC 'Children in Need' telethon it was the chimp sequence he chose. Recently, when starring in a West-End version of his show, London audiences were treated to the TV clip shown on a large screen.

The chimps themselves were later seen in the West-End not long after, when Mary and I took them to another TV recording, this time for ITV, taking part in 'Jasper Carrott at the London Palladium'. In this, Jasper's one man show from the famous theatre finished with a spoof of all those famous TV 'Sunday Night at the London Palladium' shows, with the revolving stage containing a whole host of performers. The sudden appearance of all the jugglers, dancers, showgirls and the chimps was a big visual joke on the audience as none of the acts had appeared in the show.

On this occasion we were billed as Marvin Zapatta and his talking chimpanzees. Even though we did not perform as such it was nice to be on the famous stage of the Palladium.

After the Paul Daniels recording the chimps were very tired, and sunk wearily into the straw of their travelling compartments in the back of the Landrover. Mary and I said our farewells and started the long journey back to Leicester and the circus. We reckoned it would not take us too long as at that time of night there should not be too much traffic on the roads. Indeed we made our way through London without any difficulty, but trouble was just a few miles ahead of us though.

In the world of British circus, there is an 'in' joke to the effect that the Chipperfield circus vehicles are not as good as perhaps they should be. There are numerous stories relating to the frequency of breakdowns amongst the Chipperfield fleet. Some of these are, of course, exaggerated, but even amongst the family there are favourite tales of how, on a pull-down night or other such occasions someone had trouble with a Chipperfield vehicle. The night of the Paul Daniels show was to provide Mary with one of hers.

It all started on the motorway just outside London. A pot-pourri of weird noises began to emerge from under the bonnet. Neither Mary nor I are the slightest bit mechanical and we both gazed at one another in horror. We pulled over and did a few token checks on the oil and water, both of which seemed in order. Try as we might we could not get the Landrover to start again. A sound akin to 'instant mechanical death' was all that happened when the ignition was turned. So it was that we had to call out the AA in order to give assistance. I cannot now recall what was wrong with the vehicle and all I remember is that it was impossible to mend on the spot. It was apparent that the Landrover would not reach Leicester that night under its own steam. A breakdown truck was summoned, and with the chimps still safe inside, the Landrover was winched on the back of the truck and Mary and I climbed into the cab. We settled down hoping to catch a few moments sleep before arriving in Leicester.

However, the AA Relay system is confined within county boundaries, so everytime we crossed a border we had to offload the Landrover and wait for another truck to carry us on our way. When the next truck arrived, after what seemed hours of waiting, the Landrover was again winched aboard and off we went again. As we had to cross three county borders before we reached Leicester the journey fast became a nightmare.

The chimps themselves slept through most of the journey, waking each time we stopped, but unperturbed would settle back to sleep very quickly. Mary and I had little sleep, so by the time we arrived at the quiet circus site the following morning at five o'clock we were literally shattered. We unloaded the chimps, gave them an early breakfast and crept off to our caravans for a few hours sleep.

Ours had not been the only eventful night, as what seemed like only a few minutes later, Thorsten hammered on the door with the news that during the night Assam, the tigress had given birth to four cubs. I wearily climbed out of bed and took a celebration cup of tea over to the chimps. Anna showed no sign of being annoyed at having to stay at home missing out on the television. She had spent the day with Thorsten, who she liked immensely, and had not even woken when we had returned early in the morning. I thought perhaps living with Fred she was developing his talent for deep sleep.

The experience with the Landrover reminds me of another eventful evening that was enlivened by a truculent Chipperfield vehicle. It was much later, in the summer of 1983, when I was appearing once again at the Yarmouth Hippodrome in a Jay produced show that was headlined by Mary Chipperfield with groups of horses and tigers. Our one night off a week was Sunday, and this became very precious to us. For a treat one particular Sunday we decided to take a drive out into the beautiful Norfolk countryside and find a little restaurant so as to enjoy a meal. We were joined on this occasion by Ginny Winters, a journalist and long time friend of the Chipperfield family. We had been recommended a fish restaurant some ten miles out of Yarmouth, which was in a village called Blofield. It was part of an apparently cosy old pub. It sounded ideal and we all dressed in our Sunday best. We climbed into Mary's little green Renault, having first removed bits of straw and the ubiquitous baling string and sat patiently as Mary attempted to start the car — nothing happened.

Ginny and I got out, and with encouragement from Mary inspected the engine, both of us trying to look suitably authorative. The answer, we both agreed was to give the car a push, which we did and to our delight the car spluttered into life. We got back in and set off for Blofield. Locating the said village was not easy, but eventually we found it and settled in the bar for a pre-meal drink. We chatted away and finding the need to use the lavatory I excused myself and made my way to the Men's Room. Coming back I passed the restaurant which looked remarkably empty. Further enquiries revealed it was shut. Right, we agreed to find another restaurant or pub that sold food. So into the car we climbed, and lo and behold nothing happened when Mary attempted to start it.

Out Ginny and I got, pushed again, heaving a sigh of relief when the little green demon started. We then began a search in vain for somewhere to eat. I have come to the conclusion that there is a part of Norfolk that does not eat out on Sundays. After a couple of disappointments and a couple more occasions when Winters and Hibling performed their unique car-pushing routine, we developed a technique whereby either Ginny or I would get out of the car at a pub and make enquiries inside about the possibilities of eating that night, while Mary kept the car running. Outside the fifth port of call however, Mary stalled and the wretched little car needed pushing again. Just as we we were gathering momentum, (Ginny and I were very expert at this by now) Mary's foot slipped off the clutch and whilst the car did a perfect impersonation of a kangeroo, yours truly went flat on his face.

In desperation we headed back to Yarmouth where we parked the car outside the Hippodrome and ended up by eating in an Indian restaurant not a stones throw from the circus, after having travelled a round trip of about 30 hungry miles.

The safari for something to eat was yet to come, as back in 1980, after the Paul Daniels TV recording the circus continued its tour, and as in 1979, headed for a second summer season in Yarmouth's Hippodrome. For our second Peter Jay circus several changes were made to the programme that had been on tour. We added the very strong juggling act of Rumanian Sorin Muntaneau to the line-up of speciality acts. Sorin, had a very good routine which finished with him juggling with boomerangs. The handsome young man was certainly 'one for the ladies' and became an instant friend and ally of young Thorsten. After the shows each night the two of them would frequent the town's nightclubs and discos where the would-be cassanovas made sure no female holiday-maker was unaware of their presence. As both young men had distinctive 'European' good looks they were normally surrounded by adoring female fans very quickly.

Thorsten's night time escapades often left him with a hangover, for which he received little sympathy from Mary. Worse still, if as on one or two occasions he overslept he incurred her full wrath, which at seven o'clock in the morning is very intimidating! Mary would tell him that "he was an animal trainer, and if he wanted to stay up all night, and sleep all morning he had better become a bloody juggler!". Poor old Thorsten would look suitably chastised, and Ruth and I would wink at one another and carry on working.

Other changes in the show saw Tim Delbosq take over my role as Ringmaster for the summer. Tim, son of Alfred Delbosq long-time Ringmaster of the Kelvin Hall Christmas Circus in Glasgow, was an accomplished animal trainer, and a budding plate spinner with an act that made its debut at Yarmouth during the latter half of the 1980 season.

I took over the showing of the exotic act from Carl Fischer who was taking Rosie a young African elephant to record a television series for Swedish Television. The series, a children's drama, was built around the little elephant and was a huge success with viewers. With other film and television commitments using up all the other Chipperfield elephants that summer we took only one elephant, a large African specimen, Sonya, together with her pony companion Zulu, to Yarmouth.

The routine for the exotic animals began with the elephant and spotted pony performing a short liberty routine before the familiar grouping of Highland bull, yak, camels, and Sahara the giraffe. The ring entrance at Yarmouth is fairly low, and in order to enter the ring Sahara would have to bend his neck slightly.

On one occasion he refused to leave the ring for some reason or

The Exotic act.
(David Jamieson)

other and had to be coaxed very gently by Mary and I with food bribing him to leave the ring. During this act Mary was always nearby to offer assistance.

For what seemed like an eternity he refused to exit but eventually he did, and the very patient audience gave us a big round of applause. They had been intrigued by our efforts to get the giraffe to cooperate with us and were delighted when he at last consented. It was a perfect example of the patience needed in animal training. Quite why Sahara took it in him not to leave the ring, I simply do not know, but he never refused again.

The exotic act finished with a riotous baby animal parade, which has since been high on the list of favourites amongst regular Hippodrome visitors. It was so simple, but effective, and was a perfect example of the fact that circus animals just have to be themselves and not perform anything elaborate in order to win the audiences' hearts. The baby animal parade involved young llamas, cattle, goats, a pelican, kangaroo, and Jorice an endearing Pygmy hippo.

The animals simply came into the ring and made their way out again, causing chaos in between times! The whole thing was performed at great speed, was never the same twice and the animals had as much fun, if not more than the audience. The kangaroo especially delighted in running rings around anyone who tried to catch it. In fact we planted a deliberate stooge, whose job it was to try

Jorice the Hippo with co-stars of the animal parade. (David Jamieson)

to catch the animal, miss and land in a heap on the floor, much to the delight of the audience. The pelican too, brought a touch of humour to the proceedings, and if he was in a mind to, would fly up into the gallery much to the shock of patrons sitting there!

I had great fun working with these animals, especially Sonya the elephant and Zulu the pony, who were very attached to each other. Sonya was a very gentle elephant, a steadfast performer who is now resident with the herd of elephants at Longleat Safari Park. The interesting thing about the exotic act was the way that the animals took themselves to the ring and back to their stalls again, most of the time unaided or prompted. The display featured an elephant, pony, two camels, two cattle, a giraffe, llamas, a kangaroo, pelican, assorted goats, and calves and the hippo. With only a handful of grooms the animals would often be let out of their stalls and left to themselves to make their way back into the ring where they worked, and then back home they would go — so much for critics' claims that the animals are forced into the ring. Jorice especially would know when to leave his pen complete with tank of water, charge into the ring and charge back again — woebetide anyone in his way!

It was in 1980, at the Hippodrome that the chimp act was at its best as far as circus work was concerned. Everything from the music to the costumes brought out the best in us all. Anna's impromptu stripteases and general cheekiness continually stole the show and

Sonya the elephant with Zulu the pony.
(David Jamieson)

Betsy performs her handstand. *(Courtesy Geoff Stevens)*

Betsy leaping to Author. *(Courtesy of Geoff Stevens)*

memories of that summer season in Great Yarmouth are amongst my happiest. Our circus company became friendly with the casts of the other shows in town, in particular the actors and actresses of the Robin Askwith show. We went to many parties together, and as Robin is a keen sportsman many inter-company sport competitions were held, including a nerveracking darts match. It was up to me to throw the winning dart, which by some fluke — I did! Many of the actors would join the circus folk in the Hippodrome late at night when the Flying Cherokees would erect their rigging and spend a few hours practicing new tricks. After practice was over any novice was welcome to 'have a go', climbing up the precarious rope ladder to the tiny platform, grabbing the trapeze bar and swing out over the ring and drop on the word of command from chief flyer Pete Hanson, into the net below. Many of the actors went 'flying' and even a certain chimp trainer tried it, once.

One of the actresses in Robin's company, Andi Godfrey, told fortunes and on one occasion after a party she told mine. It was very interesting and she concluded by telling me that although I was to continue working with animals, for a while at least I would not be involved with the circus. I just could not believe this, as I could not imagine myself working in a zoo again, and I was too involved with the chimps, Chipperfields and circus life. Then, amazingly a few weeks before the end of the summer season Mary informed me that a couple of interesting offers had been made to Chipperfields regarding work for the chimps and neither of them was connected with circus work. One was to train the chimps to perform their act on ice so as to appear the following summer at the Ice Drome in Blackpool; the other was to appear in pantomime in Weymouth the coming Christmas. Perhaps our fortunes are written in the stars after all?

As Mary's commitments with animals for film and television work was becoming too time-consuming for full time tenting tours, it was decided not to resume the travelling circus after the Great Yarmouth season and the company of animals and trainers returned to the Farm in Over Wallop.

The autumn provided me with the opportunity to begin teaching the chimps to ice skate, and I was helped in this by a pair of professional ice skaters at Southampton ice rink. They were able to assist in the biggest obstacle facing the skating career of the act, and that was teaching yours truly the art of ice skating. Autumn was also the time to prepare us for the forthcoming pantomime at the Pavillion Theatre in Weymouth.

The pantomime was 'Goldilocks and the Three Bears' and was produced by a certain Aubrey Phillips, a genuine larger than life figure, the epitome of the old style Actor/Manager in the Donald Woolfit tradition, and alas a dying breed. He produced several pantomimes each Christmas in his own inimitable way and, with tongue in cheek, at several other times of the year as well. He holds the distinction of being the only man to produce a pantomime for BBC 2 television, and as well as producing he often appeared on stage himself, usually as an incorrigible Dame.

The plot of 'Goldilocks and the Three Bears' is based very loosely on the old fairy-tale and has a circus theme running through it. In our production, Goldilocks is the daughter of Dame Tilly Tart, whose circus is at the mercy of the evil Demon Ringer, whose larger circus threatens to take it over unless she can some up with £1,000 which the penniless Dame is tricked into owing the evil Demon (exciting isn't it?). Happily, Goldilocks earns £1,000 as a reward for capturing three 'ferocious' bears in the forest, who also turn out to be quite friendly beasts and who agree to perform in the circus and earn Tilly Tart a fortune. After a plot to kidnap baby bear fails, the evil Demon Ringer is banished and everyone lives 'happily ever after'. Goldilocks falls in love with a handsome prince who somehow happens to get involved with the plot, as does a Good Fairy, a couple of comics, teams of dancers and in Weymouth, three chimps who appeared in a circus scene from Tilly Tart's Big Top.

Roger Cawley, in what I thought was a moment of complete madness, suggested to Aubrey that he might like to include three live bears in the plot, a suggestion which delighted the producer. The word 'live' was added to the shows' title and the plot quickly re-written to incorporate the real animals in two scenes. In one the animals performed a little routine in the 'Enchanted Glade' and another, in which the real animals were transformed by the Good Fairy into costume 'bears', (played by local children) which conveniently enabled the plot to continue and the bears to deliver dialogue.

I foolishly enquired of Mr Cawley, who was to present the bears in the epic. I was given the expected rely of "You of course!" So began my acquaintance with JR, Bobby and Dallas, three young Canadian black bears bred by Chipperfields at their safari park at Woburn. The young animals had been handled, collar trained and were very friendly, but apart from Bobby, who did a passable spot of barrel walking, they did not perform any tricks.

The three did not even sit still on seats properly and after one rather hectic rehearsal on a cold autumn morning in which Rona, Ruth and I spent more time being dragged around the practise shed on the end of leads, attached to which were three full of beans young bruins, I decided that at Weymouth I was going to need an expert assistant. Fate was kind, and it transpired that my old colleague from Dolphinarium days, Elaine Atcheler, was out of work, awaiting news of a visa enabling her to visit Australia and happily accepted an offer to work with me over the Christmas.

She came down to the Farm to assist in the training of the bears and to get to know them and the chimps. Fred, Betsy and Anna took to her straight away. I introduced her to them one morning over tea and we sat and played together. Fred was a little rough and had to be reprimanded but he took it in good spirit and was soon undoing Elaine's shoelaces, a sure sign of acceptability! Betsy groomed Elaine's hair which is the highest form of chimp flattery and little Anna gratefully accepted the offer of a cuddle. Elaine, an experienced animal handler knew that the right approach was 'friendly firmness', being open and honest with emotions and taking no nonsense from any of them. The behaviour which the chimps were accustomed to. Honesty is so important with animals. You can never lie or be false and an animal will never forgive you if you are.

The bears were a handful to say the least. There is a saying amongst circus folk that bear trainers never retire, and it is true that many trainers in the past have been injured or even killed by their charges. The difficulty with such animals is that they show little change in facial expression when in different moods, making it difficult for a trainer to gauge exactly what the animal is feeling. A trainer must therefore be extra patient and understanding.

JR, Bobby and Dallas, were far from malevolent, but their boistrousness and great strength left everybody exhausted after training sessions. In fact the 'Hibling—Atcheler' partnership almost terminated after one morning practice when Dallas nearly pulled Elaine's arm out of its socket as she was trying to keep him sitting still on his chair. I was busy at the time trying to teach JR a roll-over and shouted rather ungraciously at Elaine, "Oh, stop moaning you've got another arm haven't you?", completely ignoring the fact that the other arm was engaged in holding the lead of an equally lively Bobby. Elaine, quite rightly took offence and refused to speak to me for the rest of the day.

After a few weeks using up a lot of patience and several boxes of sugar lumps we at last managed to persuade the bears to perform some sort of routine. Although I was gambling that the panto audiences would adhere to my belief that people are happy just to see the animals and do not really expect wonders in the way of tricks. Just as well really as the animals did very little. JR rolled over, Dallas did a little dance and Bobby performed his barrel roll and took sugar lumps from my mouth. To 'fill — out' the act I introduced a little comedy whereby I laid out three hurdles in a row and announced that JR would leave his seat and very, very quickly would leap over the hurdles. As JR had not been taught to leap over anything he naturally did nothing, which as I expected brought forth a laugh from the audience.

I tried prompting the little bear with encouraging phrases such as 'Ready Teddy Go'; I asked the audience for the applause *before* the trick, even jumped the first hurdle myself, but to no avail. Of course, the more desperate I pretended to get the more the audience laughed. Eventually I would lead the bear to the hurdle and by throwing over a sugar lump he would very slowly climb over the hurdle to obtain the treat. By repeating the action at every hurdle I eventually completed the trick and we earned thunderous applause from the audience.

There was an amusing postscript to the trick however. One night, I announced that the bear would run and jump the hurdles very quickly, when he actually *did!* The sight of the animal actually doing the trick left me speechless and caused the band down in the 'pit' at the front of the stage to stop playing being helpless with laughter. Of course I realised that as we had progressed with the panto I had actually been teaching JR to jump the hurdles each night on stage. After that I had to make sure Elaine had a tight hold of his lead until I was ready for him to deliver the punchline of the routine!

If the bear act was not as strong as other such acts, I knew that the chimps could be relied upon to deliver a first rate performance. The day dawned when a little convoy left the Farm bound for Weymouth and pantomime. Roger drove a large lorry housing our props and pulling the mobile home of the chimps and bears. I followed, driving Roger's Mercedes car towing my own mobile home. It did not surprise me that we had a minor hiccup on the way when the towing lights on the lorry packed up but eventually, later than expected, we arrived at the theatre.

The Pavillion theatre is a large, modern building situated by the Harbour overlooking the beach. At the rear of the building is a little cul-de-sac normally used for car parking and it was here that we parked the caravan and animal wagons. The lorry, being dry, made an excellent storage area for straw and foodstuffs. The mobile animal wagon had three roomy compartments, two of which I gave the bears, the third one was for the chimps, although I let them sleep inside the building in dens at night. The bears, having grown thick winter coats had little chance of getting cold, but I always gave them plenty of straw at night.

It was delightful having easy access to the beach and Elaine and I took the bears for a daily run along the sands, and how they enjoyed it. We would race along the sands the winter winds behind us, feeling exhilarated by the freshness of the mornings. The bears loved to paddle and play fight in the water, and after a soaking would indulge in some more running to get dry. Many an early morning jogger, or dog owner out exercising their pet would get quite a surprise when suddenly confronted with the five of us. The bears themselves always behaved immaculately, never once getting upset with a local dog coming up to them to investigate. On many occasions local residents came onto the sands to observe their playtime.

Bears on the beach at Weymouth. *(Author's collection)*

After an hour or so on the beach we would rush back to the trailer where the bears would have a hot bowl of rice cooked with milk and sugar. The bears proved great company, not in the same social friendliness of the chimps, being more robust, dog-like companions. Only on one occasion did their good manners slip and a quarrel break out on stage between JR and Dallas as they were being transformed by the Good Fairy into 'friendly' bears. It was all very brief, but very loud and for once the 'ferocious bears' of the forest were very convincing with their parts. Renee Bourne Webb, the lovely actress who played the Good Fairy was not at all put out by the snarling and growling animals and in true showbusiness tradition carried on reciting her lines, albeit considerably louder than usual.

In between their two appearances on stage the bears waited in the wings as the gap was not long enough to warrant us returning to the trailers outside. I had worried that the fifteen minute or so wait would result in the bears becoming bored and restless, but they behaved so well, sitting with us as we played and petted them, remaining quiet until they had to go on stage again. Whether coming to the theatre from their wagon, or returning again, the bears would rush at top speed and Elaine and I held onto their leads as best we could. I must admit, on occasions one of the bears would slip loose, but they never ran anywhere except to the stage door, or back home where they would sit and wait for the rest of us.

The chimps had only one appearance in the show, save for a scene-stealing bow from Anna in the finale, when they appeared in the circus scene, supposedly coming from the Tilly Tart Big Top sharing the 'performance' with the illusion act of Paul and Danny Denver. It was odd adapting our circus ring routine for a stage show with the audience on one side only and on one occasion I can remember bowing to a bemused stage crew in the wings. The chimps were soon contemplating on how to use the new performing area to their advantage, Fred delighted in whipping the band below him during the whip cracking routine! Anna was totally amazed at being on a higher level for once than her audience, and during the first few days of the run would rush up to the front of the stage and peer out over the audience. All three chimps, on three separate occasions, provided some very amusing moments that winter. Anna scored a big triumph when she visited a local pub one lunchtime, and took over the proceedings, including pulling pints for regulars. The pub, the Duke of Edinburgh, was run by the charming Mick and Ulla Terry and had become a favourite meeting place for the company after the evening performances. As the Landlord and Lady had been so kind to us I promised to bring the chimp along before we left town. Her one and only visit to a pub was captured on photograph, copies of which were eagerly sought after by the company.

Fred decided to go on strike one afternoon shortly after Christmas, causing chaos both on and backstage. No sooner had Dame Tilly Tart (played by the charming actor Lex Daye) in an outrageous Ringmistress's outfit introduced us, Fred turned his back on the audience and refused to work, sitting the entire act facing the backcloth. I was totally surprised as he had never shown any reluctance to work before. He was not ill, or apparently upset, but here he was refusing to work. In the confusion that followed I did my best in the circumstances, with the stalwart Betsy filling in for Fred on certain tricks, but the act was about three minutes shorter than normal. In any show, timing is essential, and the panto was no exception. Paul and Danny Denver who apart from their illusion act, also proved expert actors as Demon Ringer and Simple Simon respectively. Directly after the chimp act the two of them had an acting scene on stage, but as they performed their illusion act before the chimps worked, it was very quick costume and make-up change the two undertook whilst the chimps were performing.

On the day of the strike I came off stage still slightly bewildered by Fred's actions and as I was returning to the dressing room bumped into Danny Denver, calmly making his way to the stage thinking he still had plenty of time before the chimp act was finished! The funny thing was he saw Elaine, the chimps and I, said "hello" to us all and walked on for a few seconds before it dawned on him (and us) that the stage was empty! Poor old Danny rushed on stage full of panic, and alone! Paul, his partner in the next scene was calmly applying the finishing touches of make-up unaware that Danny was desperately ad-libbing on stage, until he heard through the dressing room intercom a decidedly anxious Simple Simon, pleading "Boys and Girls, have you seen the Demon Ringer? Shall we call him? That's right, nice and loud! Louder! I *think* I can hear him coming!"

Enter one out of breath Demon.

However, it was Betsy who caused the biggest excitement. Late one night she managed to open the door of her sleeping den, and off she went on an exploration trip around the theatre. Elaine and I were returning from the Duke of Edinburgh and I remarked to Elaine that someone had left the auditorium lights on inside the building. At first I thought nothing more of it, but then feeling uneasy I alerted the night watchman and the three of us entered the building to be greeted by a sheepish looking Betsy, who had turned on every single light switch she could find.

Relieved that she had not done any damage to the building I took her back to her den, scolded her light heartedly and put her to bed. It was only the following day that we realised that turning on the lights was not the only exploit that Betsy had got up to during her midnight escapade. As the musicians took their places to begin playing for the afternoon matinée performance, to their horror they found that pieces of their manuscript had been sabotaged, ripped to pieces and it was not difficult to guess who was responsible. For the first time I regretted ever teaching Betsy the paper tearing routine. Understandably the musicians were not too pleased, and someone's joke about 'the monkey obviously was a music lover' did not help smooth tempers.

However, the paper incident apart, the animals were taken to the hearts of the company, especially Aubrey Phillips who, whenever he greeted the chimps, always presented them each with a bar of Peanut Brittle, a great favourite.

Aubrey was delighted with the response the animals earned from the audience and critics. One local newspaper stating that the 'Animal magic, made the show a panto not to be missed' and '. . . judging from the children's faces it will be the animals' contribution that most will remember.'

To this day, Aubrey has continued to involve real animals in his productions, and has thought up ways of including, dogs, bears, goats, pigs and even tigers in the plots of his shows.

Many of the company would join us on our morning exercise on the beach, especially Brian Weston, who was besotted by the animals, and Laura Nayman, the pretty young lady who played Goldilocks. Laura herself made a brief sojourn into the world of circus when in 1983 she was the Singing Ringmistress for Sally Chipperfield's Christmas Circus in Birmingham.

Star of the panto was ex Black & White Minstrel regular Dai Francis, who was making his first panto appearance playing the Inn Keeper. He bravely posed for photos with the chimps on the very first day of rehearsals, and from the look on his face he must have wondered just what he had let himself in for, signing a panto contract!

Following the four weeks at Weymouth, we agreed to add the bears and chimps to future spring productions of the panto being staged at Bradford, Norwich and at the historic Wimbledon theatre. Elaine left for Australia shortly after Weymouth, and a new assistant was needed. Help was very close at hand as Brian Weston offered his services. He was an excellent choice, the animals already knew him and more important they liked him, especially Fred who would love to cuddle Brian. Fred, had been known in the past to test people he met by showing off or being uncooperative waiting to see what their reaction would be before becoming friendly, yet he never did with Brian. I am sure the chimps' ease with Brian stemmed from the fact that he is such a nice person, modest, quiet, and instantly puts everyone at ease.

For the rest of the panto tour our line-up of performers both human, and animal was altered slightly. Mike Holloway, the singer and actor took over as headliner and made a dashing, romantic Prince. Mike was joined on one occasion by Fred, when singing a solo. We were waiting for our act when he promptly ducked under a backcloth and joined the Prince in his Palace, creating an unusual duet.

On the animal side we lost Dallas who went away to do some filming, and was replaced by a tiny little bear cub called Bassie, who became a show stopper and competed with Anna for scene stealing. He was much too young for a collar and lead, and after a little stagefright initially, he would bound on to the stage with great gusto, causing havoc with his playfulness. On one occasion he almost robbed Goldilocks of her wig as she lay 'sleeping' in the forest, the catastrophe avoided by the quick-thinking of the Fairy Godmother and skilful manoeuvring of her wand.

Bassie stayed with me in the caravan, but in Bradford where there was no room to park wagons outside the lovely old Alambraha theatre, the animals were housed at the side of the stage in portable dens. I had no choice in this case but to take Bassie to my digs. Happily I was staying with an old friend, Jean Raper, who with her family welcomed Bassie with open arms. Just as well, because Bassie took over the household. He demolished several cherished houseplants, broke a couple of family heirlooms, argued with the family pets, but such was the charm of the little fat bundle of fur that no one could ever scold him. Jean's family all argued as to who it was that would give him his regular milk feeds, despite the fact that in his eagerness to reach the contents of the bottle he would scratch like mad.

Bassie slept in a converted cat basket, and even travelled to and from the theatre in it — on the bus. He gave one inquisitive bus conductor a shock when I enquired if, as my animal was neither a cat nor a dog, I had to purchase a ticket.

In the theatre it was a constant battle with Lex, Brian and myself versus Bassie with regards to possession of the shoes in the dressing room which we all shared. He was such a happy little animal, and was gently tolerated by the older bears, and even the chimps with whom he played. Everyone who met him was won over by his appeal, including Tommy Steele whom we met whilst we were at Bradford. During our stay at Bradford we were given an extra night off, as Tommy was booked into the delightful old theatre as part of a nation-wide concert tour of Great Britain. All the sets and backcloths used for the panto had to be taken down after the evening show the night before, ready for the concert tour crew who would come in very early the next morning and rig the complicated lighting and sound systems used in the Tommy Steele show.

Of course, none of the animals could be moved from their quarters just to one side of the stage, a fact which caused Tommy Steele's Road Manager to nearly have a heart attack. "Tommy will go mad!" he snorted, and insisted that the animals be moved out of the theatre. I did my best to calmly point out that the cages had been built up specially in the wings and could not be moved anywhere.

The clearly upset Road Manager was now convinced that the presence of three bears and three chimps would result in his instant dismissal from the Steele entourage, and made it quite clear that the animals presence would probably mean no performance by Tommy. I was now convinced that Tommy was unreasonable, must surely be something of an ogre, and therefore enquired if the Road Manager thought Tommy would expect me to sit on the pavement outside, along with my three chimps, and three bears until the concert was over? Eventually it was decided that rigging should go ahead as usual and as soon as Tommy Steele arrived we would discuss it further. The Road Manager walked away muttering to himself, and from across the stage in the wings, Betsy gave out an extra large hoot as if to emphasize the gravity of the situation.

All morning I fretted about the meeting with Tommy Steele, who, I convinced myself, must surely be a spoilt star. Whilst exercising the animals I rehearsed a quick speech making sure I would tell him that I would remain with them all the time, that we would not be in the way, and that they would keep quiet during the actual show. Although short of actually committing murder I was not quite sure how I would achieve the last promise.

Eventually a message came across the intercom backstage to the effect of summoning me to the No. 1 Dressing Room — Mr. Steele had arrived. Here we go, I thought. I made my way to the dressing room, knocked sheepishly on the door and went inside. Before I could utter a word Tommy said, "I hear you've got a baby bear do you think I could see it please?" He then added "I love bears!" I fetched the little bear and as he played, Tommy and I chatted about the animals. Tommy's eyes sparkled as I told him about the chimps and he was obviously genuinely interested in the animals. Tommy went as far as to ask if the chimps could actually appear on stage with him that evening and a routine was devised. I was so relieved to find that far from being an ogre, Mr. Steele was in fact extremely charming.

In the concert Tommy had a little chat with the audience about half way through the performance. Members of the audience had earlier been asked to write down a question for Tommy to answer during this spot, and it was here that the chimps were to make an appearance.

As the show started, I sat with the chimps keeping them occupied whilst Tommy and the very talented company went through their paces on stage.

Shortly before the interval we got changed and as the second half of the show began we crept to the wings ready for our entrance. Our cue was to enter as soon as Tommy asked if there was any more questions and on we strolled, the chimps bearing their questions on cards. As

Tommy had anticipated, the arrival of the 'Kids' on stage brought a big howl of surprise from the audience. This turned to laughter as Tommy reached for the card which Betsy was holding only to have Betsy rip it to little pieces, "That's my Contract" murmured Tommy. Fred handed his card over with his customary dignity and Tommy read the card, "Ask me what I think of the show?" so, Tommy did, and Fred responded with his gesture of tapping his forefinger on his head in a 'crazy' expression. As we made our exit to our applause Tommy was kind enough to give the panto a plug, and he also mentioned that he had met little Bassie. I put the two chimps back in their quarters, rewarded them with some fruit and feeling confident I foolishly thought that I could creep up to the back of the auditorium and watch the rest of the show.

I sat watching the fine performance and all was well, until Tommy brought the lights down and seated at a grand piano began softly to play the opening bars of the beautiful song 'Bridge Over Troubled Water'. All of a sudden the mood was shattered by an ear-piercing scream, drowning out the music. Obviously a squabble was taking place over food in the chimp quarters. I could have died on the spot with embarrassment, but happily Tommy just stopped playing, and laughed. When all was quiet he raised crossed fingers and began playing again. I rushed to the chimps and sat with them until the show ended.

After the concert ended Tommy told me how thrilled he was to meet the animals and he thanked me for letting them appear on stage. Tommy Steele was really genuine and it just goes to show one should never judge people before you meet them.

After Bradford we went on to Wimbledon and Norwich. At Norwich the Theatre Royal is situated next door to a lovely park where we exercised the animals each day. The chimps were delighted to play in the trees and it was a joy to watch them swing through the branches with so much agility. The chimps would wait until one of the company who had joined us on our walk, or myself had our attention diverted and wham!, they would jump on us from a great height. Sometimes I would go on my own to the park with just Anna and Bassie and it would be bliss to stretch out on the grass and watch as the two young animals tumbled about with endless energy, exploring every nook and cranny. On one occasion uprooting several geraniums from an immaculate flower bed, which I hurriedly replanted before any park keeper could spot the act of vandalism!

At Norwich we made a whirlwind tour of television studios one afternoon, first climbing aboard a taxi and making our way to the studios of Anglia Television to record an interview for the 'About Anglia' magazine show. Then dashing over to the BBC studios with only seconds to spare so as to appear on the 'Look East' magazine show. At both studios the chimps were treated to tempting food and drinks, and I thought that all the spoiling would effect our evening performances, but the chimps, despite all the excitement of the day, worked as well as ever.

The 'About Anglia' slot was especially fun, with the presenter of the programme, Christine Webber entering into the spirit of things and dressing like us in yellow dungarees. The tea-party was chaos, with the chimps making a great deal of noise and a great deal of mess. Christine and I tried to keep a sense of dignity mostly in vain, although I later learnt from Christine that she was offered a job on the strength of her chimp interview, for it was thought that if she could keep her head with three mischievous chimps, she could handle anything!

The press were again kind to the chimps, calling them 'real troupers' and saying that 'they stole the show' — never work with animals if you do not want to be upstaged it seems!

The last port of call for the pantomime ensemble was Wimbledon where the vehicles were parked on a school playing field some five hundred yards away from the theatre. This necessitated a walk to and from the theatre twice a day in costume to pick up the animals — I got some strange looks I can tell you!

There was also the problem of finding electricity, it being holiday the school was all locked up with no access. So armed with my supply of cable and a great deal of cheek, I set off towards a row of houses that bordered the playing fields. I knocked on a door and enquired of the lady who answered, if I could plug into her electricity supply. I had taken Anna with me and it was the little chimp that won her over, so much so that she not only agreed to let us plug into a socket in her kitchen, she also refused payment.

The last show of the tour came and went, and I was very sad that it was all over, I had made some good friends working in the pantomime, and I had learned a great deal too. We all said our goodbyes and went our separate ways.

The bears were going to a quieter life at Longleat and the chimps and I returned to the Farm to resume our skating lessons, ready to make our debut in 'Showtime on Ice '81' at Blackpool.

As I drove back to the Farm I reflected on the many similarities between panto and circus. Both are magical worlds, capable of totally involving children in a simple, unsophisticated way that can hold its own even in a world of videos and computers. Above all, they are both bastions of good clean family entertainment and as such should be cherished.

Chapter 6

Mary Chipperfield's Skating Chimpanzees

Teaching the 'Kids' to ice skate was amongst the most fascinating episodes in my time with them. Perhaps the most interesting point to consider is that, in all honesty, it was not really me that taught them to skate, rather it was the patient instruction from two professional ice skaters, Len Ligget and Bernard Eddy. Len and Bernard were instructors at Southampton's ice rink, and were delighted to accept the challenge of teaching two chimps, and their trainer to skate ready for our debut in Blackpool in the June of 1981.

We had begun our initial training in the autumn the previous year, our schedule interrupted on two occasions, firstly the pantomime tour, then a little later when we joined Austen Brothers' Circus as special guest artistes at the start of their 1981 tour. Austen Brothers, run by three very talented brothers, Brian, Patrick and Michael together with manager Peter Featherstone is a very efficient, mobile outfit, extremely self contained with the brothers and their loyal staff, being able to turn their hands to anything. They even made their own Big Top.

In 1981 the show was expanding slightly and decided to 'borrow' the title Jimmy Chipperfield's Circus World for the tour, with Mr Jim becoming President of the show, and several animals from the Chipperfield organisation joining the circus. The 'borrowing' of another circus' title is common practice in Europe and the USA, but is something seldom done in this country, possibly because, with a few exceptions, circus dynasties in this country do not become household names like their foreign counterparts.

As guest artiste with the Austen show I was made instantly welcome, becoming very quickly part of the team, and the few weeks with the circus I can honestly say were amongst my happiest tenting experiences. Today, the Austen Brothers' Circus has reverted to its original title and is still going strong, presenting the public with good solid traditional circus entertainment. Its company still make me very welcome whenever I visit the show.

Back on ice, things were improving slowly but surely. The first hurdle to overcome was getting the chimps used to wearing shoes, something they had never done before. Anna, being too young to cope with wearing skates, was not going to learn anything new for the act, although with the aid of several layers of warm clothing and thick woolly socks she was going to make an impact.

For a few weeks before we actually went near the ice, I spent a few hours a day playing with Fred and Betsy, introducing them to pairs of old skating boots. Eventually I slipped them onto their feet together with pairs of old socks and tights which they would have to wear when we were on ice. Fred had a passion for shoes and feet, which on occasions bordered on being kinky! He loved to smell peoples shoes and if anyone approached him barefoot he would shower their feet with sloppy kisses. He was delighted therefore that we were actually indulging him in his fetish.

Neither of them objected to the boots or socks, it was another example of their faith in me as their mentor/providor. As long as I approved of what was going on, and was supportive, my confidence gave them the incentive to do anything. With this in mind, it was essential that I mastered the basic skill of ice skating myself before introducing the animals to the ice rink. Therefore at the same time as the animals were getting accustomed to the boots, I would make a very early morning journey from the Farm to the Southampton ice rink, some 20 miles away, where either Bernard or Len would coach me. The early morning sessions were necessitated by the fact that heavy demand was made on the ice rink by professionals and amateurs alike, and also because I had a lot of work back at the Farm during the day.

I must admit that I was terrified at the prospect of learning to skate. My stomach churned over as I drove down to the rink that first morning, but the fear of failing and incurring the wrath of Mary spurred me on! Len and Bernard were very kind and patient with me on those early lessons urging me on slowly, never getting cross and praising any slight improvement on my performance. I knew they would make good chimp trainers. Anyone who has ever been on ice knows that the hardest thing to overcome is the fear of falling over. Once I had fallen (yes, I fell over lots of times) the fear began to leave me and confidence crept in slowly. The first time I was able to skate across the rink, reverse, and turn on one blade totally unaided gave me a great thrill and sense of achievement. The more I grew at ease with myself, the more speed I was able to achieve and moving quickly over ice is an exhilerating experience, almost indescribable — a bizarre combination of speed and coldness.

As soon as I was confident enough to move about on the ice without assistance we decided it was safe to introduce the chimps to the ice. At the Farm I was still encouraging Fred and Betsy to wear the boots, standing up in them and adjusting their balance with the weight on their feet. This was no hardship for them but I wondered how well they would take to the ice, if at all.

Mary accompanied us on our first morning, and it was important that everything went smoothly so as to give the chimps as much confidence as possible. We arranged that we should be at the rink even earlier than normal for we knew that the chimps would arouse much curiosity from other people in the building. We wanted any fuss kept to a minimum, so we figured the earlier the start the fewer the number of other learners there would be. We never did use the ice when members of the public were present and throughout the training sessions the only other occupants of the ice were sportsmen and women training for competitions, and youngsters (some very young indeed) receiving professional tuition.

After the initial shock of sharing the rink with simian skaters everyone settled down to normal. The chimps learning their routines hardly raised an eyebrow from the others also practicing hard. I often thought it very amusing to see Bernard or Len skating up and down the rink with one of the chimps, only feet away from a young lady or gentleman learning blade control or a new spin. Everyone at the rink did take an interest in the chimps progress of course, and when not on the ice themselves they would sit and watch the chimps and break into spontaneous applause when the animals mastered a new trick or skating movement.

The first morning we let the chimps explore the rink before taking them onto the ice. The coffee bar met with great approval and a vending machine that issued chocolate became a habitual stopping place, both on the way in and out of the building. We carefully introduced them to Len and Bernard and were relieved that the delight of the introduction was mutual. Fred and Betsy developed a great deal of trust for the two gentlemen, especially Len whose father-like approach was greatly appreciated by the 'Kids'. Bernard was more extrovert in character, and once Fred and Betsy had mastered the basic techniques became a great playmate with them. Fred would constantly pester him to take him for another spin around the ice, hooting with delight. In the initial stages, the calmer Len won great admiration from Betsy in particular, for his quiet approach to what was after all as far as Betsy was concerned a serious sport.

Fred was also very impressed with the never-ending supply of biscuits from Lens' pocket. In our first lesson we did nothing more than lace the boots up and place the chimps on the ice, Mary and I holding them firmly to give support while Bernard and Len made encouraging noises.

Fred in his usual bold fashion, scrambled onto the ice to investigate this new, unusual environment, and promptly decided ice was for eating. Betsy, not so confident as her partner, clung very tightly to me, not at all sure about the way the floor was slipping under her feet. The first lesson ended after a few minutes and we retired to the coffee bar for warm drinks. Fred took a great interest in the skaters on the rink and sipped his tea whilst staring out of the window.

Following our first day I felt it would be easier for all concerned if I took the chimps down for their lessons individually, allowing us to spend time on the chimps' little idiosyncracies. Bernard or Len took it in turns to oversee proceedings and under their instruction Fred soon developed a great interest in the new game becoming very keen to progress. Betsy took longer, and only really enjoyed it all as her confidence grew. With both animals the training routine would begin with me holding them under their arms and easing them forwards. Len or Bernard would skate either in front, encouraging them or especially in the early stages, behind me to ensure that I did not slip whilst holding the chimps. I knew if I slipped whilst holding Betsy any precious confidence she had developed would be shattered. Ebullient Fred was not so fragile.

In reality the chimps did not have to skate at all in the accepted sense. All momentum was provided by me. The chimps for their part, had only to master their balance on the skates and I would do the rest. Fred actually did teach himself to skate after a fashion, and would propel himself unaided along the ice at quite a speed. Betsy never achieved such mastery of the skates, but once she perfected her balance and felt at home on the ice as I predicted, she became a powerful asset to the act and it was her that contributed the most spectacular tricks.

As the weeks went by we adopted new positions, with the chimps holding onto my hand on one side and either Bernard or Len on the other. This system proved very successful for Betsy, but with Fred it only had the effect of encouraging him to lift both feet off the ice and expect us to participate in the chimp-invented game of 'carry Fred along the ice'.

Little by little the chimps found their balance and we reached the stage where both animals could stand up on ice unaided, then take hold of a cord and be propelled along by me.

All this activity spanned several months, with each session approached as if it was a game. More than ever I had to refrain from scolding the chimps in case of shattering their confidence.

Once the basic techniques had been mastered we set about teaching the tricks that would constitute the routine. By now both the older chimps were attending each session on the ice with Anna putting in the occasional appearance. Again Anna, by virtue of her size, was a hit with the staff and pupils at the rink. One morning though she demonstrated a rather loud vocal tantrum after a squabble with Fred, and she somewhat evaporated her projected image of sweetness and light.

Mary and I devised a simple routine for the chimps, working with the principle that simply seeing them on ice would be a novelty and impress the most critical of audiences. Therefore we decided against any real spectacular acrobatic tricks. Obviously the easiest thing for us was to adapt tricks already performed in the standard circus act for use on the ice. Accordingly Betsy's hurdle jumps, the swing routine with Anna and Fred, and Betsy's somersault were transferred onto the ice.

The full routine as performed at Blackpool was as follows:—

Chimps on ice.
(Author's collection)

Author with assistant Perri and three chimps. *(Author's collection)*

The spotlights would come up revealing us all in a pose on the centre of the ice. We would then make a quick circuit of the ice before Betsy and Fred skated in figures of eight around me and an assistant. Betsy then leapt three hurdles, before Fred provided an anti-climax by ducking underneath a fourth larger hurdle. Betsy regained our credibility by performing three somersaults followed by the swing routine. Fred brought the act to a close by staking a large circle on an increasingly longer lead, becoming faster and faster and waving a Union Jack flag as he did so. The last trick was very effective and usually had the audience clapping along with the music.

This also proved an example of Fred's intelligence. In his enthusiasm he would often wave his flag so fast that it would fly out of his hand, but this would not break his concentration or momentum. Instead he would manoeuvre himself into such a position so as to pick up the flag on the next circuit and resume waving.

He also discovered that he could send me 'flying' across the ice in similar fashion to his flag if he stopped suddenly. To propel Fred in the last trick meant a great deal of effort on my behalf, skating furiously in a small circle. Should Fred stop suddenly I would fall very unceremoniously on my backside, giving Fred and the audience a great deal of pleasure.

Fred would only sabotage the act's grand finale at irregular intervals, lulling me into a false sense of security, thinking he had forgotten all about upstaging me when "Wham!", on would go his brakes and off I would go again.

In retrospect I think we should have changed the routine we performed as it threw away our best trick of Betsy's hurdle jumps right at the start. We should have saved that for the end of the act. Still, we were all new to the game of ice skating and with the exception of the fellow members of the cast, there was no one at the Ice Drome to advise us. Nevertheless, as far as I was concerned the chimps had performed marvels at adapting their act for the ice and I was so very proud of them.

It was obvious that I was going to need an exceptional assistant in the act, someone who would not only be able to cope with the animals but also ice skate too, and it seemed an impossible request. Then, as has so often happened in my career, fate stepped in and lent a hand, bringing Perri Banham right to our doorstep. Without Perri, I do not think I would have coped with the season at Blackpool. She became more than an assistant being a firm friend and ally.

Perri, a young school leaver had been obsessed with ice skating from an early age and had decided that she would turn professional. She had been training at the ice rink at Southampton, the port being her home town, and incredibly, she had been offered a job as one of the chorus in the Blackpool show. We asked her if she would consider the extra task of assisting me during the act. Perri readily agreed and began rehearsing with us.

She was very nervous of the animals at first, and on one occasion, having witnessed their temper tantrums, I am sure she made a mental note to cancel the contract. However Miss Banham has a very strong will and once she makes up her mind to do something, come hell or high water she will plough on. To make matters worse, the chimps sensing her nervousness, did their best to make her life unbearable by constantly ignoring anything she asked them to do and looking up at me as if say, "Who *is* this woman?" It was impossible for me to leave them alone with her at first as she had no command over them at all. I must admit I had my doubts too on occasions as to whether or not the chimps would ever accept her and perhaps we should have to find someone else. The Banham determination is something not to be taken lightly however, and with time her confidence grew and she became firmer with the three rogues, learning to understand their gestures and moods. Led by Anna on this occasion the 'Kids' began to warm to her and with relief, I knew all was going to be well.

Perri proved to be a great asset to the act on ice. She was obviously the better skater by far, certainly the most attractive (a stunning blonde) and as time went by she sold the act well, learning to smile and 'compliment' — the theatrical term for the subtle 'asking of applause' by an act's assistant. In the first few weeks of the season when the chimps and I were still a little wobbly it was Perri that often

Perri with Betsy and Anna (in arms). (Author's collection)

held us all up when we skated around the rink.

Perri worked very hard in the show, as apart from helping in the act by assisting with dressing the animals which, because of the boots was a tiresome, drawn out job, she also skated in every production number in the show continually executing skilful skating movements — it is no wonder she complained of being tired every so often.

When she first started to rehearse with the chimps she was still very much a young teenager fresh from school. It was interesting to see how as the season wore on she transformed into a responsible young lady, developing a distinct personality. It was her first job, the first time she had lived away from home coming from a very close-knit family and she handled it all very well — with a little help from Fred, Betsy and Anna.

Both Perri and I were greatly helped by the staff of the Ice Drome, I was especially indebted to the maintenance and wardrobe departments for their help and support regarding props and costumes. The ladies from the wardrobe often shared their morning tea-breaks with Anna, and many of them would stand outside the chimps' living wagon and watch them play. I was also pleased by the number of technical staff who would find the time to come and see the show on numerous occasions to see the 'Kids' work.

In the show itself the members of the skating company were very kind to the novices. In fact working on the ice show was at times very

Author with Betsy and Fred on the ice rink. (Author's collection)

similar to working in a circus, such was the atmosphere. The more experienced chorus skaters were all too ready to pass on tips to Perri with regard to make-up and costume. Several of the soloists gave me extra skating lessons which was an enormous help. I used to practise a little everyday on the ice, and even perfected a small leap into the air — although I did not add it to the act.

The 1981 production of the Blackpool 'Showtime on Ice' was very spectacular. The Ice Drome itself, situated in the heart of Blackpool's Pleasure Beach Amusement Park is not the most attractive of buildings, but each year a very creditable ice show is produced that could hold its own anywhere in the world of professional ice skating.

In the show that year was a very funny trio of comic skaters, 'The Jackpots' — local lads who had worked hard to earn international recognition. All three young men were expert skaters who used their talents to make the comedy look very easy. Providing another speciality was the illusionist duo 'Ricki and Roddi' who had transferred their mystifying stage act to ice a few years earlier.

Amongst the show's production numbers were a cockney tribute to London, a voodo sequence and a number built around the song "All that Jazz" in which the piano player, miming away on a mock piano in the middle of the ice rink looked very similar to the chimp trainer.

The stars included the solo skaters Jacquie Harbord and the handsome American Ron Green. Towards the end of the show the two champion skaters had a duet which I always made a point of watching as seeing anyone who has achieved such high standards in their chosen profession is always such a joy. Ron won the heart of one of the chorus skaters, Mandy Childs who had become a great friend of Perri and I. As can be expected, everyone in the show took a keen interest in the romance and we were all delighted to learn of their marriage shortly after the season had finished.

Sadly, despite all the happiness of the season on ice, I had to face a slight tragedy that marred the whole summer at Blackpool. Halfway through the rehearsals the running order of the show was changed, and as a result, much to my chagrin Perri was unable to assist in the dressing of the chimps. She had to have a quick change from a production number costume into the one she would wear for the chimp act. Foolishly I accepted the offer of help from Yvonne Parks, a lovely lady and assistant to the producers of the show and a 'mother' figure to all the girl skaters.

Yvonne was beyond any doubt an animal lover and someone who had had experience with animals, both at the ice rink in Blackpool on a previous occasion, and apparently with chimps in another ice skating extravaganza in the Middle East. I thought she would be ideal to help and it was obvious that the chimps liked her, they hooted with delight every time she came into the dressing room to assist with dressing the chimps with their boots. She always rewarded everyone with sweets after the task was completed.

So, it seemed my problem was solved and indeed all went well until one evening in July. Yvonne came into the room as usual, helped me with fixing the boots onto the 'Kids', then she bent down to say "Cheerio" to Anna, when suddenly, without warning Betsy flew at Yvonne's back. In order to protect her head she raised her hand and Betsy sank her teeth into Yvonne's finger, and as it happened my hand too as I had thankfully, acted quickly enough to come between them.

Betsy withdrew as quickly as she had begun the attack and indeed it was all over in seconds. Yvonne fled the dressing room in tears, and I had to go straight onto the ice and work, in quite a state of shock not really knowing the extent of the damage caused to our friend. Both Perri, who had now joined us, myself and the chimps went through the act not really knowing what we were doing, just going through the motions. As soon as we had finished the chimps returned to their quarters and I rushed to the office to see what was happening.

Yvonne had gone to hospital where it transpired she had lost the very tip of her middle finger. (Ironically, the hospital said if it had been kept on ice it could have been sewn back. All the ice in the show and nobody had thought of that!)

Poor Yvonne was very shaken, as was Betsy who remained subdued for several weeks. I was very down at heart, and I can remember tearfully confiding in Mandy Childs later that night that "everyone was going to think ill of old Betsy, and she isn't a nasty chimp", I insisted.

Betsy had never shown such aggression before, or since, and to this day I do not know why she acted as she did. Perhaps she was jealous of Anna, thinking she was getting an extra sweet, perhaps she was protecting Anna from Yvonne, thinking she was somchow attacking the little chimp? This I think is more probable, as for the first time in their presence Yvonne was wearing a mock fur coat and possibly as far as Betsy could tell, when Yvonne had her back turned it may have resembled an animal that was 'smothering' Anna, and so leapt to her 'defence'. This would explain why Betsy did not persist in the attack and halted immediately she came to her senses. Perhaps above all, the incident emphasized the unpredictability of chimpanzees. Loving them is easy, understanding them is harder.

As I expected the Management did consider withdrawing the chimp act, but it was gratifying to see the company, including Yvonne herself, spring to the chimps defence. We were not sacked, and thankfully the season passed without further mishap.

The best thing to come out of our ice skating exploits was recognition from world skating star Robin Cousins and a guest appearance a couple of years later on his 'Skateaway' TV series.

In 1981 Robin had been touring the United Kingdom as special guest star in the renowned travelling ice show 'Holiday On Ice'. This ice extravaganza was appearing in the Ice Drome a few weeks before the resident summer show opened and our rehearsals began whilst the holiday show was still in the building. Robin watched the chimps rehearse and even skated with the chimps on a couple of occasions. Subsequently, when searching for something unusual to provide some light relief in his 'Skateaway' show he approached Chipperfields, to see if one of the chimps could appear with him at the Bristol Ice Rink where the series was being recorded.

By this time the chimps had not skated for quite awhile, living in semi retirement, and I feared that they would have forgotten how to skate. As only one chimp was needed I decided to take Fred with me down to Bristol. I had previously visited the rink myself to brush up on my skating as I had not been on the ice for quite awhile either.

We need not have worried about Fred though, even after the lengthy absence from ice he performed with great panache, showing he had not forgotten any of his old skills. In fact he was very excited when confronted with the familiar sights of an ice rink. He hooted with pleasure as we brought out his socks and skates and then eagerly took Robin's hand and mine, and skated into the spotlight.

Robin explained to the television audience that the natural 'bow-leggedness' of chimps meant that their bodyweight was always held dead centre, making them ideal skaters. They were unlikely to fall over whatever they did on ice as their wide stance gives them good balance. Robin confessed that after the years of skating he was a little bow-legged himself! Robin related how impressed he was with skating chimps he had seen in the past, and he was obviously delighted to have Fred's company, and Fred behaved so well.

The 'Skateaway' series was designed to encourage people to take up the sport and I am sure Fred was responsible for several new enthusiasts to skating following his appearance on the show! The series came after the chimps had more or less retired from public life. Chimps live to a great age, with circus animals normally out-living their wild counterparts, thanks to the cossetted lives they lead.

After the age of nine however, chimps can become unpredictable, adolescence making them difficult to handle! Some circus chimps carry on working throughout their lives and I have seen some animals in American circuses still working at the age of 30 which is very old for a chimp. Animals in the Chipperfield organisations however are retired whilst still young enough to be integrated into the various chimpanzee colonies established in the Chipperfield safari parks and other such establishments.

At the end of the Blackpool season it was suggested that the chimps might benefit from retiring. It was to be a very painful decision for me to make. The animals were such an integral part of my life I was loathe to let go, especially as the chimps were performing better than ever. Their act on ice achieving critical but more importantly, public acclaim. Outside pressure on my personal life also indicated that a move from the chimps might be necessary, and indeed the last few weeks at Blackpool were an unsettling period.

As the season drew to a close it was decided to retire the animals, and I became very sad at the prospect of losing them. I knew I would no doubt see them from time to time, but our lives together would never be the same, and besides, if they were to integrate into a colony they would probably not want to see me again.

The last few days at Blackpool hung over us all like a dark cloud, the three chimps knew things were changing, sensing my depression, and I was dreading the last show. Yet emotion had to give way to the practicality of their departure. I honestly felt I could not drive them back to Longleat Safari Park where they would go before a decision was made as to which group they would eventually join. I knew they would be going to somewhere familiar, see well known faces of both humans and indeed chimpanzees, of whom all three of them were fond. I told myself that I would probably get in the way of their settling down, and yet as the transport arrived to take them away I made them a final cup of tea, I felt for all the world as if I was somehow betraying them. I bade them farewell with all the guilt of a traitor.

With the passing of the chimp act I had decided to leave 'circus' at least for a while and I had sold my caravan to Perri, who was to use it when she worked the following Christmas as a skater with 'Holiday On Ice' in London.

My animals and mobile home now gone, I hung around the site where we had parked for our Blackpool season, then heart heavy I got into the car and drove to Cheltenham where I was to move into a house and rethink my future.

I drove in silence, not being able to remove the animals from my mind. Were they all right? How were they taking the journey? Had they had another drink? After a few hours I pulled into the nearest service station for a cup of tea, and lo and behold in the car park was the familiar red and blue Chipperfield wagon containing the chimps. I rushed over to see them, and of course they were all right, treating this journey like any other they had experienced in their career. They were not even surprised to see me of course. I was pleased I had seen them and I watched the lorry and trailer leave with a more cheerful heart.

I arrived in Cheltenham where a new house and home occupied my time. I kept in daily contact with the Chipperfields to see how the chimps were settling. "Stop worrying, they're fine!" was the reply, but like a parent whose children had left home I did worry. They would not join a group right away as that would take time, but for the present they were living together in a roomy enclosure in the park's pets corner.

I awoke many mornings in the weeks after leaving the chimps and found myself absent-mindedly making the chimps their tea, a habit which took ages to break.

I did not know then, but I was not to be parted from them for too long, and shortly we would be working again in the spotlight. There were to be a few more performances from the Mary Chipperfield Chimps before they finally retired. I will end my book with those events, but before I do I would like to dwell for a few pages on the subject of performing animals in general, and hopefully answer the allegations that are sometimes levelled against circus animal trainers.

Kitti Roberts' performing dogs with Author. *(Richard Foster)*

Chapter 7

Performing Animals

The United Kingdom has long been regarded as a nation of animal lovers and therefore should be proud of the many respectable societies and charities (we shall forget the less respectable ones) that devote themselves to animal welfare.

I am always surprised, when from time to time some, though not all of these societies, make allegations concerning circus cruelty. It seems odd to me that the circus, whose whole function as a form of entertainment is surely to present magnificent animals in the peak of condition, should be accused of subjecting animals to loss of dignity. Indeed even the RSPCA has now made it their policy to ban *all* performing animals, although many inspectors 'in the field' are by no means anti-circus. A year or so ago the Society placed a well constructed advertisement in most national newspapers which depicted a sad-faced lion wearing clown make-up and hat with the headline, 'Circus is no fun for animals'. This produced the desired emotive effect, even if such a sight to my knowledge has never been seen in a circus anywhere in the world.

The RSPCA was also involved with one of the most controversial issues concerning British circus. They provided a considerable grant to a human-only 'circus' which was the brainchild of members of the Hassani family. The show, started in 1979, was said to be a direct result of a wish by the late celebrated clown CoCo (father of Tamara Hassani) to see a circus run without animals.

This apparent wish has been quoted time and time again by those opposed to circus animal acts, but I find it hard to accept that this famous old clown, (who once had his own dog act and who for years was associated with Bertram Mills Circus, whose standards of animal husbandry was world-renowned), could be against performing animals. Still, one would assume that the beloved entertainer's daughter knew her father's desires better than the rest of us. Although it must be stated that CoCo's other daughter, Olga, wife of the late great lion trainer Alex Kerr, has always denied that her father had any such notions about performing animals.

By all accounts the Circus Hassani did not fare too well on tour, but is still in existence today surviving as an attraction in an amusement park with a second unit — a zoo! Where of course, the public can see plenty of animals.

In 1984 Gerry Cottle, with a blaze of publicity launched a non-animal circus cited by the various animal rights groups as the 'circus of the future'. Many circus folk, myself included felt let down and were saddened by Gerry's decision. Gerry toured the show in London and elsewhere but late in 1985 the circus's General Manager, in a statement to the theatrical newspaper 'The Stage' revealed that "....... the experiment had not paid off, we have proved that in spite of Gerry Cottle's good name, a very good show and some wonderful press and television coverage it hasn't worked. People came up to the Box Office and asked what animals we have, when we tell them we don't have any, they walk away. We are simply forced to put animals back in the show". The public, it seems likes its circus traditional.

For the winter of 1985/86 Gerry put on a show at Camden Lock in London, which was visited by Princess Michael of Kent and her family. The show featured Gerry's elephant act, Peter Harrison's sealions, exotic animals and Liberty horses from Mary Chipperfield's resources, presented by David Sherwood, and Suzanne Chipperfield riding High School. All animals in the peak of condition, healthy and fit.

It is the condition of circus animals that constantly defeats so many of the arguments against circuses and explains why the majority of the public are still in favour of performing animals. As soon as anyone enters the Big Top, they can see for themselves how well cared for the animals are.

Still, the accusations continue to be thrown at the circus, and recently we have seen militant animal rights groups, including the frightening Animal Liberation Front, adopting the call to ban circus animal acts. Some of these groups are becoming increasingly violent to obtain their objectives, especially as most people disagree with their views.

Animal Rights campaigners, in various disguises have decided to make life as difficult as possible for circuses. Gandey's Circus has recorded all the incidents it has experienced in 1985 at the hands of protestors and it makes alarming reading; circus personnel have been verbally and physically threatened, circus property has been destroyed or damaged. Unbelievably, bricks and others objects have been thrown through shop windows displaying circus posters, and shopkeepers threatened with renewed violence if they display posters again!

Many, more organised groups stage 'demonstrations' outside circuses, taunting the public as they visit the show with their families and often damaging cars parked by patrons whilst their owners are inside the Big Top enjoying the show. Sadly, many of these so-called animal 'lovers' claim to represent the RSPCA.

Happily, the public has shown no sign of wavering in their support for us, if anything the tactics adopted by protestors strengthen public resolve to visit shows.

Some groups of 'antis' (the collective noun given by circus folk to those against circus animal acts) manage to persuade local authorities to ban circuses from council-owned land. This lawful action is much-favoured by the self-appointed 'watchdog' over circus animals, 'The Captive Animals Protection Society'.

A ban usually comes about in the following way. A circus will visit a town, (and it *will* only visit a town if there is a demand) and be enjoyed by thousands of ratepayers, who will see no reason in writing a letter of support to their council regarding circus visits. Yet those *against* circus will write letters listing all the misdeeds supposedly committed by circus trainers to their animals, not only to the council but also to the press.

Having created a one-sided situation, pressure will be put on a council to discuss a ban. Often the circus is not represented at such meetings, and the first the transient circus learns of a ban is when one is placed.

When the circus can put its case the result is often positive, but about 40 councils, including the former Greater London Council, have banned circuses from their land.

In practical terms the ban is rather ineffectual. Circuses can of course still visit towns which have imposed bans, simply by finding private sites, and after a time these private sites become established and local people forget that their council has ever banned circuses. This fact led to several councils in 1985 reversing their bans. However a ban does damage the good name of circus artistes, and circuses therefore must, and do fight them.

Whether or not the criticism of circuses stems from the militant animal rights groups or from a society like the RSPCA the complaints seem to be twofold. First that the training and day to day existence of our animals involves mental and physical cruelty, and secondly that it is somehow immoral to have animals perform for us.

The question of cruelty is an easier one to answer than whether or not it is 'right' or moral for animals to perform in circuses, so I will answer that first.

Anyone who has trained a pet dog to walk to heel or to sit on command has grasped the 'secrets' of the animal trainer. Bertram Mills, the circus director, once said that the essence of animal training could be summed up in three words — 'Patience, Understanding and Reward'. He was right. Before anyone can begin to train an animal he or she must have a complete understanding of it, both its physical and psychological make-up must not be a mystery to the trainer. In the Soviet Union all circus artistes, including the animal trainers attend circus schools to learn about their chosen career. There are no such schools in the UK and perhaps there should be, as I do not think it would be a bad idea if a budding animal trainer or groom had to attend courses/lectures concerning animal husbandry.

Nevertheless, any animal trainer of note will endeavour to find out

Liberty horses at Circus Knie.

(The Swiss National Circus)

all about his animal, how it works, how it feels and reacts to different situations. I myself, spent every opportunity just observing the chimps at play and it was at these times that I learnt most about how they thought and how their individual characters differed. I read everything I could lay my hands on that had been written about chimps, I discussed aspects of chimp behaviour with people who had previous experience of working with them, eager for tips and advice. All of this provided me with a strong background which I could draw on when training and caring for the 'Kids'.

Training begins the second you come in contact with the animal. It is not just a matter of teaching the routines in the practise shed or circus ring. The daily chores of feeding, mucking out and grooming play a part in the training process, which is why it is so important that a person training an animal should have constant daily contact with it.

Ideally, it is best to start with young animals, those who have been weaned and having left 'mum', are full of life. Any young animal, whether it be a chimp, tiger, elephant or horse is playful and in the initial stages, training is a form of organised play. This approach to training, as if it were all a game, as you will have seen, works well with chimps and enabled me to teach Fred, Betsy and Anna all the things they performed in the circus. Surely then, common sense will dictate that happy animals perform far better than ones which are cowed or dull-witted with fear?

Most people will have some idea how dogs and horses are trained for work with man. After all there is little difference between circus dogs and horses and sheep or guide dogs, police horses or showjumpers. Only the most ardent 'animal-libber' would complain about dressage horses, like those from the Vienna Riding School, horses which perform the same movements as circus dancing horses. They are trained in the same way, only the presentation is different.

I dare say the average sheepdog would rather sit in front of a fire on a cold winter's day, than go chasing sheep over the hillside, but if he is asked by the shepherd to do so, out of love and respect he will. I have yet to hear anyone say that the shepherd is guilty of cruelty and of forcing the dog to perform against his will. Yet some maintain that the only way a circus dog is made to perform is by gross cruelty.

Mary Chipperfield's magnificent English Arab liberty horses were all handpicked from various studs up and down the country. Before any circus training commenced with regards to performing a routine the horses were 'trained' to adjust to their new life. They learned to be handled, to familiarise themselves with bridles and harness. All this was achieved with patience and over a long period of time. By continual association with the animals, through feeding, cleaning or simply by just talking to them, the horse (and for that matter any other animal) begins to accept the individual humans around them. After awhile they will allow themselves to be touched and stroked, then more often than not, they themselves will initiate contact with their new found companions.

By hanging bridles and harness in the vicinity of the horses, they will soon accustom themselves to the smell and sight of the tack, and with patience they will allow the trainer to place the tack on them. This will never happen if the animal has no faith or confidence in the human. Only when a horse is accustomed and happy with the harness can anyone think of beginning to teach it a circus routine. The first step is to simply lead the animal into the ring and let him familiarise himself with the sights and sounds, encouraging him with a titbit or soothing word.

To reach this stage will have taken weeks, and the process is a similar one for all circus animals, although obviously requirements alter with different species, a sealion for example does not need a bridle.

Liberty horses, as the name suggests work in the ring without riders, receiving their cues from the trainer via a whip or voice command. Normally they work in troupes numbering from two to sixteen and as such must work as a team and will therefore be stabled within sight and sound of one another.

Like the chimps, the horses ready to learn their circus act will begin with an ABC of basic tricks and commands. The most important is learning their position in the file of animals as they trot around the ring. Other tricks taught as an ABC normally consist of walking forwards and backwards and stopping on word of command, trotting and galloping to cue and breaking file to come to the trainer.

In training horses and other such animals an assistant is vital. The grooms will be known to the horses and in the early stages will walk with the horse as it makes its way round the ring. The groom will attach a lunge (a length of rope) to the bridle and will lead the animal through the movement indicated by a gesture from the trainer which is either a voice or whip command. For example to teach a horse to pirouette (turn a circle on itself and continue walking) the trainer will cue the animal and exactly at the same time the groom will gently lead the animal through the action.

This is repeated time and time again until the groom, after a few weeks will become aware that the animal is performing the required movement itself and not relying on him. The groom will then unclip the lead and the trainer will cue the animal to see if the horse will respond independently. If the result is negative the groom will return and the process will be patiently repeated until the horse connects the movement with the trainer's cue.

The trainer never uses the whip as a punishment, but as an extension of his arm. For example, in teaching a horse to break file and come to the trainer in the centre, the groom will attach the long lunge to the bridle and he himself will stand behind the trainer in the centre of the ring. Whilst the horse is trotting around the ring the trainer will gently flick the end of the whip on the horses belly (a trainer will be expert with a whip, knowing how to use it long before working with the animals) and call him by name. As he does this the groom will gently coil the lunge, bringing the horse to the centre and to a reward. Again, after a time the horse will connect the whip cue with the desired movement, and the groom and lunge can be dispensed with, but not the whip. I cannot stress too strongly that the whip is not an instrument of punishment but merely an aid. I can remember when working with Mary how I was made to have whip practice. Empty drink cans were lined up on a wall and only when I could touch them with the end of a whip without them moving was I allowed to use the whip with animals.

Horses are trained in short regular intervals, patient repetition being the key. Just how long the process may take depends on how bright the individual animal is, or indeed how bright the trainer. Once a liberty horse has gained the rudiments of the ABC training he will then start to work with the other members of the troupe. Usually, they are introduced to each other slowly, perhaps working in pairs for a while before finally the entire troupe is brought together. Then, the intricate patterns and formations can now be taught. To my mind, a well-matched team of liberty horses, all wearing fine harness and plumes is one of the most breathtaking and beautiful sights to be seen in a circus ring.

No matter how complicated the trick performed by the troupe the pattern of training is the same. Beginning with the groom/lunge combination responding to the trainer's whip or vocal cue with the animals thinking for themselves eventually and responding without any prompting.

The one element of training which is the most important is the reward for a movement correctly performed. If the animal fails to respond correctly it is not punished by a beating, nor is it rewarded. The process is simply repeated until the desired effect is achieved — and that can take a long time.

Just as human athletes need time to train to become fit, so circus animals must be afforded time in order to achieve certain tricks. A horse walking on its hind legs (purely an extension of a natural movement) has to have time to gradually strengthen its muscles before it can perform such a feat.

The majority of circus animals are of the domestic variety, horses and dogs being the most obvious examples, but even animals like elephants, camels and llamas have been domesticated by man for centuries. There is a very thin line between 'domestic' and 'wild' animals as far as the circus is concerned. Even the so called 'wild' animals, the lions, tigers and bears will have been bred in the circus, zoo or safari park, probably being fourth, fifth, perhaps even sixth generation performers. Chipperfield's Circus (the original, run by Jimmy Chipperfield's brother Richard) once bred 40 lions, tigers, and leopards during one season alone!

Some people though, are quite happy to see domestic animals perform in circus, but remain unconvinced that the so-called 'wild' animals can be taught by any method other than one which involves cruelty. In many respects the training of lions and the like is similar to that of circus horses. Both the horse and lion trainer has to spend countless hours with his young charges. He feeds them cleans their quarters and by doing so will eventually be accepted as part of the animals' social group and will be treated accordingly. Training can now commence. As with the horse the young lion will be allowed to explore the ring cage, investigating the props positioned therein and soon feel at home.

With lion or tiger acts the customary approach is to teach the entire group of animals which make up the act at the same time, rather than individually. For the first few lessons the animals do nothing more than romp about in the cage, but before long the trainer, with the aid of a piece of raw meat on the end of a stick will bribe them into sitting on a pedestal. The animals are rewarded and praised when they remain on the pedestal, but reprimanded vocally when they vacate without being asked. Training has now begun in earnest.

The animals learn that they are expected to sit on a particular

Sally Chipperfield's lions at Yarmouth. *(David Jamieson)*

pedestal when ever they enter the ring, and soon begin to recognise the times when they can play and when they must work. The routine for the act will have been worked out, most probably built around a natural ability to leap. To teach a big cat to jump through a hoop of fire is relatively simple. With the incentive of a piece of meat on the stick you encourage the animal to leave its place and jump up onto a larger pedestal set in the middle of the ring. Rewarded with a piece of meat, another one is used to tempt him back to his original seat, making sure that he follows the stick as he does so.

This routine is repeated for a few days until the task is being performed with ease. Next, instead of rewarding the animal with the meat on the second pedestal the animal is coaxed into jumping a small distance (say a metre) before receiving the reward.

Each day the distance between the third and second pedestal is increased until the animal is leaping the length required. Gradually a hoop is introduced, placed between the two pedestals, and after the initial hesitance, the lure of meat is usually enough to tempt the animal to leap through. From here there is one small step of igniting the hoop, although as a trick the fire-hoop is becoming a rarity in modern circus. The animal leaps through thinking no more about the flames as does the household tabby when he sits at the fireside.

Most trainers, although not all, substitute meat with vocal praise during performance but the stick remains, as a cue, not a weapon. The late Carl Fischer Snr would dispense with an actual stick and cue his animals with a conductor's baton, a pencil, and even on occasions — a feather!

Of course such animals are potentially dangerous, and if upset or surprised could do incredible damage to their trainer, and yes, trainers have been killed by their charges. Jealousy can occur with male animals regarding their trainer as a rival in the fight to win attention from females, and a lion or tiger may then challenge the human in their midst.

The modern-day trainer is far removed from the old image of the Lion *Tamer* of the Victorian menagerie who would subjugate his animals by any method available. This was not in any way a serious attempt to teach them anything but merely to allow himself access to the cage to thrill an audience with his 'courage'. Today however, critics would still maintain that wild animal acts appeal to an audiences' bloodlust, such as in the case of bullfights! I think this is doing circus audiences a grave injustice. Circus goers appreciate the skill of the lion trainer in establishing a close working relationship between a man and animal. They admire the partnership in the same way as those who attend sheepdog trials admire the shepherd and his dog as they work in harmony.

I have never seen a circus audience react to the sight of a lion or tiger in any other way except admiration and appreciation of the beauty of the animal. I have never seen anyone laugh at a circus animal, many a time they might laugh *with* them, but that is something else entirely.

In any profession there is good and bad. It would be naive to think that there has never been bad trainers, who whether through ignorance or spite, ill-treated their animals, both in training and in the day to day care of the animals.

Yet must we punish all trainers for the deads of unidentified wrong doers? Everybody knows that in our community pet dogs are neglected and cruelly treated, and yes one way to stamp out this abuse would be to prevent everybody from owning a dog. I know of animal rights campaigners who would support this motion, but surely most of us agree such extreme measures would be unthinkable. Then it must follow, that the banning of circus animal acts is also an extreme measure and in the long run very unfair?

One of the all time favourite circus performers is the elephant, and no other animal arouses more emotion from the 'antis'. To them the elephant is the symbol of the so called loss of dignity 'suffered' by the circus animal. Yet, the Asian elephant in its natural homeland has been a domesticated animal long before it was ever considered for work in the circus ring. In India today the elephant is a vital part of religious ceremonies far more elaborate than the average circus performance!

Author training with young elephants. (David Jamieson)

Whilst it is the Asian elephant most commonly used in circus, it is true to say that the African specimen has been seen on occasions. The plight of the African elephant in the wild is well documented. Its habitat is constantly under threat from man who needs more space, more farm land. Through no fault of its own, rather through mans' greed and selfishness the elephant is regarded in some parts of Africa as a pest, and many thousands have been culled, quite apart from the numbers poached for ivory. Sometimes young animals that otherwise would be culled, are offered to the world's zoos and circuses. (Admittedly some would offer the opinion that the animals would be better off dead, but I wonder if the elephants would agree?)

These youngsters need careful handling, obviously frightened when they first arrive at the circus, but they are very responsive to human contact and being very intelligent are quick to establish a relationship with their handlers. Their training is similar to that received by the horses, taking a little longer to win confidence, especially with the African species which by and large is more nervous than the Asian counterpart. In the circus older elephants already trained are often used to reassure the newcomers, a method employed by Indians in the teak forests. The process of repetition and the use of assistants helping the animals respond to cues is still applicable.

Circus Hoffman's baby African elephants. *(David Jamieson)*

Bobby Roberts elephants at the Seaside. *(Courtesy Richard Foster)*

On travelling circuses elephants are housed in tents, tethered to special boards by a front and back leg. This method has led to criticism as it is stated that the elephants are too restricted, remaining on the boards except for performances. In well run circuses this is not the case as the animals would have regular exercise, training and rehearsal periods, quite apart from performances. The rest of the day is filled with grooming, feeding and sleeping. When Gandey's circus featured the large, gentle Indian elephant Ranee, one of Mary Chipperfield's animals, they allowed the animal to spend the entire day grazing around the circus site in the company of the show's own camels, llamas and ponies.

Certainly, one should never stop attempting to improve in animal husbandry, and circuses do experiment with new methods of housing their animals. Circus Hoffman's baby African elephants, rescued from a cull in their native country are housed untethered in an enclosure, with access to their transporter if they so wish.

The failure of elephants to breed in captivity has often been ascribed to the unsuitability of a zoo or circus environment. More often this lack of success is due to the fact the many establishments will not keep bull (male) elephants, for when a male enters 'musth' during the mating season he has a tendency to become aggressive and unpredictable. I will agree that the keeping of all female herds does little to the cause of preservation, although some zoos have experimented with artificial insemination. Interestingly enough

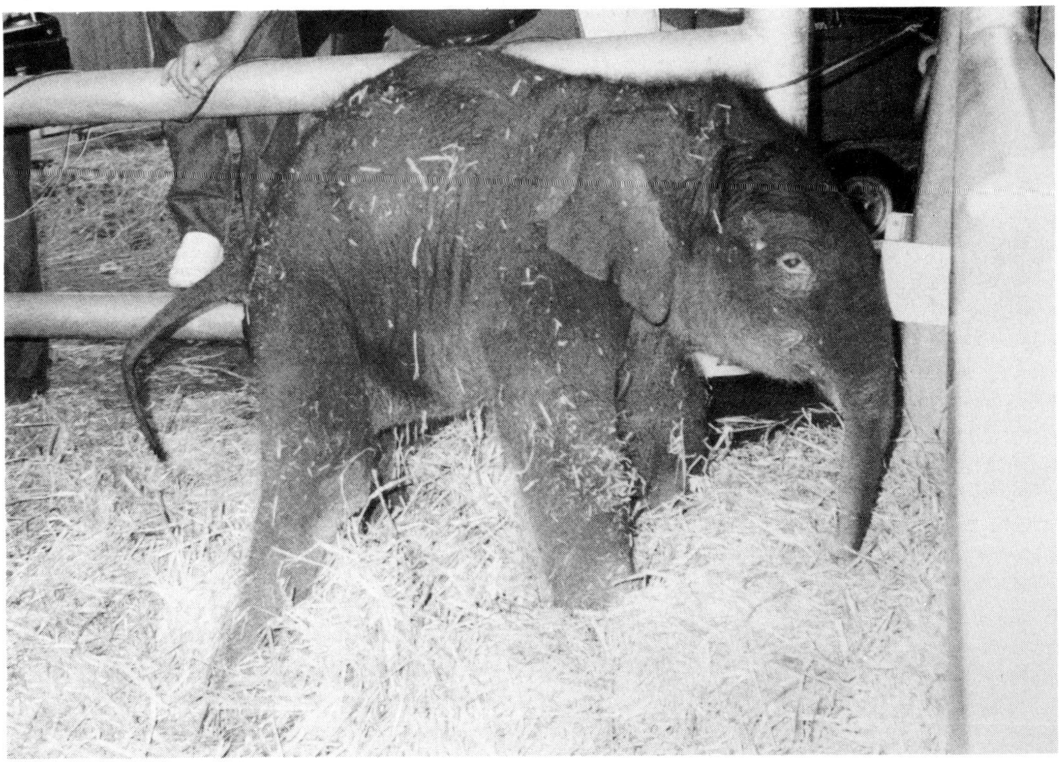

Elephant calf Lohmi, 30 minutes after birth in 1985. *(Courtesy Chris Krenger)*

circuses have bred elephants, with the Swiss national Circus Knie being particularly successful. Their current herd includes Sahib a magnificent bull born in 1963, Madura born in 1965, and Lohmi born in 1985. Would it be fair to assume that the parents of these animals were content with their lot? More recently the Knies were involved in helping to organise the integration of Chipperfields magnificent Indian bull elephant Maxi (of Princess Anne fame) into the herd of elephants in Zurich zoo. It is pleasing to report that Maxi was responsible for fathering a baby elephant born a couple of years ago.

It is essential that we do not fall into the trap of anthromorphism in our approach to animals. A circus elephant cannot tell us in words whether or not he is 'happy'. We must use expert knowledge of animal behaviour learned from study of wild and captive animals to successfully gauge how content circus animals are.

With this in mind it is nonsense to imagine a lion gazes out of his zoo or circus cage dreaming of a life in the open spaces of Africa. Today there are few, if any lions in circuses that have ever experienced the hardships of life in the wild. Rather like their parents and grandparents the circus is their environment, the one in which they feel secure.

Let us not forget that life for any wild animal is one constant struggle to survive, many constantly face hunger or thirst, having to roam vast distances in order to obtain their basic needs. It is open to conjecture whether or not the animal enjoys roaming miles in search of food or water, but certainly here at home, wild birds and animals readily set up residence in city gardens, preferring to take advantage of a provided food supply rather than search for themselves!

Certainly, a wild animal is never bored, something which might be a problem for a captive animal. In this respect a circus performer is lucky, leading an active life, with training keeping it mentally alert. Most enlightened zoo directors do advocate 'occupational therapy' for the animals in their collection. In other words, training.

The relationship between trainer and animal has often been studied by zoologists. The eminent Swiss zoologist Dr Heini Hediger made a detailed study of the Chipperfield leopard act when it toured Switzerland with Circus Knie, and one trick, when a black panther leapt into its trainer's arms particularly impressed him. He wrote ". . . . Only complete mutual familiarity and trust makes possible such a leap. The panther springs onto his trainer from a distance of several metres. This is a most unusual, at present certainly unique, taming achievement. The panther must feel he will make a comfortable and safe landing, while the trainer must have the assurance that the panther will not use his claws. In the panther's circus environment the trainer thus represents neither prey nor tree trunk, but a partner to be taken care of". From 'Communication between Man and Animal' (Image Roche).

The circus panther's life is perhaps far removed from that of his cousin in Africa or Asia, but is the quality of his life any poorer? No one has yet convinced me that it is.

No animal can perform a trick that does not correspond to a natural movement. It is the animal's natural appeal that causes thousands of people worldwide to visit circuses. A horse rearing on hind legs, a monkey balancing on a pole, the panther leaping, these are all extensions of natural behaviour. In his book 'The Animals Report' in which the circus is criticised, Richard North cast doubts on Richard Chipperfield Snr's knowledge on elephant behaviour after Mr. Chipperfield had stated that elephants could perform tricks like standing on their heads, because "they sometimes do similar in the wild".

Shortly after reading 'The Animals Report' I happened to watch the television documentary concerning the elephants who visit the Kitum Caves in Africa. The elephants visit the caves at night, and in pitch darkness go miles underground to obtain minerals and salts. Using special cameras, the film unit recorded scenes of the animals excavating in the rocks. It was amazing to see the balancing and acrobatic movements that the animals used in order to obtain the salts and minerals. Nothing so difficult would ever be asked of a circus

Author and Betsy demonstrating her natural balance. (David Jamieson)

Performing elephant. (Simon Finlay)

animal, and indeed, one individual reaching down into a gully performed a movement very akin to standing on its head.

If it is accepted that an 'unnatural' (for want of a better word) life led by circus animals is not harmful, it is still difficult for some to believe that it is 'right' for a circus animal to perform simply for human amusement. There is no straightforward answer.

For thousands of years man has utilised animals either as a food source, for sport, clothing or simply as companions. As a point of interest if we are to ban circus pigeon acts, then must pet budgies disappear also? In Britain today there are countless numbers of animals kept as farm stock or as pets, far more than the comparatively few used by circuses. Anywhere animals are kept there is a danger of abuse and of course all decent people must keep an eye out for cruelty wherever it may occur. There are some however, who will not rest until they have created a society where man has no dependence on animals in any shape or form. Not only do they wish to see circuses disappear, but also farm animals, guide dogs and pets. They are entitled to their views of course, and if they wish to become vegans, wearing clothes made of man-made fibre only, and withdraw from the companionship of animals, then all well and good.

Nevertheless, if the majority of people feel justified in keeping animals in society, I cannot see that if animals are found morally acceptable in the role of clothing and feeding us, run races for us and act as eyes for our blind, any reason why they should not entertain us.

There are laws to protect animals in circus. The RSPCA and for that matter any individual can prosecute a circus for cruelty to animals. In 1965 when the subject of animals was debated in the House of Lords a Home Office spokesman said:

"Your Lordships may perhaps feel that it is significant evidence against allegations of cruelty that the RSPCA do not appear to have brought any successful prosecutions for cruelty to performing animals although the protection of animals act 1911 gives them sufficient basis for such action."

The RSPCA were themselves party to the 1925 Performing Animals (Regulation) Act, which itself would probably not have come about had it not been for the efforts of circus boss Bertram Mills. His son Cyril comments in the book 'Bertram Mills Circus — it's story',

"If he (Bertram Mills) resented anything it was the wholesale and indiscriminate attacks made by some animal protection societies against everyone connected with circuses. He knew that animals could be and were being trained without cruelty in circuses, and elsewhere and he did everything he could to demonstrate the truth of this, but at the same time he was the first to agree that if there were black sheep in the circus fold they should be rooted out and prosecuted and it was in large measure due to his untiring efforts that the Performing Animals (Regulation) Act was passed in 1925."

Elephants taking a break. *(Richard Foster)*

Elephants being transported on Robert Bros. Circus. *(Courtesy Richard Foster)*

Since 1925 all animal trainers have to be licensed by the Home Office, and all establishments where circus animals are exhibited or trained have to be open to inspection by the police or a veterinary surgeon approved by the local authority.

In 1965 the Association of Circus Proprietors gave the RSPCA an open invitation to visit circus premises, at any time without warning, to inspect animals, an offer which holds fast today. I have always welcomed the RSPCA any time that I have been working with animals and have enjoyed many an afternoon's chat with an inspector over a cup of tea, discussing animals.

The Association of Circus Proprietors acknowledge the fact that there could be more legislation regarding circuses. I think all true circus people regret the fact that anyone can grab a few ponies and a tent and call themselves a circus, a situation that could lead to animal abuse, and also the type of entertainment offered is not worthy of the name circus.

In lieu of legislation the ACP has its own strict guidelines. Three vets, Doctors Taylor, Greenwood and Scott meet twice annually to set standards for member circuses. They make surprise checking visits, interviewing staff and trainers and of course inspecting animals carried with the show. In the last couple of years the ACP has made it policy that only performing animals, or animals in training should be travelled with a circus. The days of exhibition animals in old style menageries have disappeared. Member circuses must also carry exercise cages, large practise cages built up during the day with access given to animals such as lions and tigers.

The self-imposed standards set by circuses belonging to the ACP means that the modern-day circus is continually improving, a fact that is recognised by many city councils who will only let land to circuses belonging to the Association.

Personally, I think that the old romantic notion which created an air of mystery surrounding the circus has hindered understanding of the treatment of circus animals. The circus must in the face of criticism be more open to the public, by saying, "This is how our animals are trained, this is how they are housed, exercised, fed etc. What is wrong?" Thereby putting the 'antis' in the defensive chair. In the past the circus has been called upon to defend itself from the 'antis' only after an allegation of cruelty has been made.

There is a difficulty in getting circuses to project a united front even through the ACP. Most Circus Directors have a hard enough time keeping heads above water, just operating a travelling show against a tide of rising costs. Constantly on the move, communication between various outfits can be poor, and there is the question of professional rivalry to be considered.

Some of the circus 'old school' still find it hard to believe that anyone could even think of criticising circuses for using animals. I did

Louis Knie performing with one of his Bengal tigers. *(Circus Knie)*

hear one old circus director saying that the public would lose interest if they knew how circus animals were trained — the mystique would be gone. Nothing could be further from the truth, and in fact the opposite is true. It seems nowadays people like to understand the ins and outs of a subject, and understanding the mechanics of a task only increases their appreciation. I think this is true, not only of animal acts, but also the acrobatic ones too.

This has been successfully demonstrated by the many circuses who now open the daily training sessions to the public. In Britain morning rehearsals and training on Gandey's Circus is always witnessed by interested individuals and school parties. During the training, a commentary is given by Gandey's house trainers, the accomplished Martin Lacey and David Sherwood. Despite fears expressed in some quarters, by allowing the public access to the circus during the day, attendances have not fallen for performances, in fact quite the opposite.

Gandey's Circus works extremely hard to put the record straight about the way animals are trained, with Carol Gandey and Graham Cottle taking every opportunity to invite interested parties to see the animals at work and play.

When I first worked for Mary Chipperfield as tiger groom, she was adding new animals to the established act and thanks to a fine summer was able to hold her training sessions in a ring cage built up in the open-air. Mary could not have prevented anyone from witnessing the training even if she had wanted to. It was interesting to see people from the towns we visited coming time and time again, taking an interest in individual animal's progress.

I only hope the Association of Circus Proprietors can encourage more trainers to create better understanding of their art amongst the public. For the last few years the Association, which itself was founded in the 1930's by the leading circus proprietors of the time to foster good relationships between circuses and the public and also between shows themselves, has had as Secretary the very hard-working Malcolm Clay. He is tireless in his efforts to promote quality circus and whose honest, steadfast approach has earned him great respect both in and out of our profession. In particular Malcolm is responsible for making sure that the circus gets the opportunity to have a voice whenever it comes under attack, either in the media or at council meetings.

The Circus Fans Association is a group whose members are people from all walks of life who are linked by an admiration for circus, also does much to counteract allegations of circus cruelty. It publishes a superb quarterly magazine King Pole (named after the main poles of the Big Top) edited by David Jamieson, a photographer of note. It was largely due to his efforts that the June 1985 edition was entirely devoted to performing animals.

Entitled 'Animals in the Circus — A King Pole Special' it contained articles and photographs relating how circus animals are trained and cared for. Copies of the magazine were distributed to local councillors, Members of Parliament, the media and even Royalty. It was very well received.

1984 was the Golden Jubilee year of the Circus Fans Association, and in the same year a new pro-circus lobby was born. The 'Circus Society', brainchild of David Price and Bernard Bale, stated that its aims were to 'further the interest of circus as we know it' and I am delighted to report that it is doing just that, campaigning hard on behalf of real circus. The Circus Society complements the work done by the ACP and the CFA, and it is encouraging to realise that there are many people prepared to fight to ensure that animals are retained in circus performances.

The circus as we know it began with horses, when in 1768 the 'Father of the modern circus' Phillip Astley, an ex-military man gave displays of horsemanship in a roped-off circle at Halfpenny Hatch near Waterloo Bridge in London. Today, over two hundred years later circus people continue to work with horses, and other animals, not just because it is a business or a way of life, but also because they choose to, because they happen to like animals. They are justifiably proud of a unique rapport that they have with them.

I will continue to be amazed, that despite often admitting to having doubts on just how much they know about the training and care of circus animals, societies and individuals class circus trainers, like myself, in a similar category to the old bear-baiters or cock-fighters. Yet, there is nothing to suggest that circuses can be equated with such barbaric practices, and perhaps history itself suggests that the demise of such exhibitions may have been hastened by the arrival of the circus, where the developed skills of human and animal performers could be enjoyed at close quarters.

Above all, the question of circus cruelty is personally hurtful and offensive. If someone maintains that circuses are cruel they are therefore insinuating that I, as a circus animal trainer, am cruel. I admit to many faults but cruelty is not one of them. It seems sad and pointless that thousands of pounds are wasted in an effort to persuade the public not to visit the circus by attempting, albeit unsuccessfully, to prove that circus animals are maltreated, whilst all around us genuine and proven cruelty to animals does indeed exist.

Chapter 8

The Ringmaster

Within a few weeks of the chimps leaving me at Blackpool there came a request from Austen Brothers Circus, with whom we had worked earlier in the year, to see if the chimps would be available for a Christmas Circus they were staging at the Gloucester Leisure Centre. Roger Cawley rang me from Longleat to see if I would consider working the act once more. With the Christmas season only a few weeks away, I argued with myself that the chimps would not have embarked on any retirement plan. Gloucester was very close to my home, I was not doing anything else at Christmas, it would be fun working with the inimitable Austen show again, and I *did* miss the chimps, so I accepted.

Within a very short time Christmas was upon us and I found myself at Gloucester awaiting the arrival of the chimps. Nothing in my life will be as rewarding as the greeting the three chimps showered on me as they arrived at the Leisure Centre. They were tired after the journey, but their vocal recognition was enormous, and it came as they heard my voice, before actually seeing me. I opened the door of their wagon and was bowled over by the three occupants and we sat cuddling each other, the three chimps doing their best to out do each other in their enthusiastic grooming of their friend!

After they had finished greeting me, and everyone else they knew on the circus they settled down inside the building for the night, tired and dusty. The transformation overnight was amazing. As I arrived early the next morning their delight at returning to a circus environment was obvious to all. Troupers that they were they seemed overjoyed to be back in familiar surroundings, and they performed the act with great gusto. It had been many months since they had worked the full circus routine, but they did not put a foot wrong. We had a great three weeks together.

At the close of the Christmas season I decided that I had been foolish after the Blackpool season not to have accompanied the chimps back to their Longleat quarters. So after Gloucester I drove them back to the park which nestles in the Wiltshire countryside, and which would be the temporary home for the chimps until it was decided which chimp colony the three would join.

There were three more occasions when I worked with the chimps before they finally retired. One occasion was the Robin Cousins 'Skateaway' programme, another time was with Betsy in a week of 'Old Time Music Hall' while the third and final time was when all three chimps joined me on a Channel 4 Wales Christmas circus, staged by Gandeys and transmitted as 'Syrcas Cymru'.

I had decided to try my hand at an acting career. Just why Hibling, who had more in common with Barnum than Shakespeare should imagine he was able to become a talented thespian he did not know, but there you are. Chipperfields did offer me the opportunity to work with other animals perhaps eventually some more chimpanzees, but I declined feeling that in a kind of way it would be unfaithful to the 'Kids'. Also, I foolishly thought that my life would now be in theatre and I would leave circus behind. In the final analysis that was very short-sighted of me and I was soon to find out that once sawdust is in your blood, it *never* lets go of you!

However, I was not thinking about that when early in 1982, Michael Napier Brown, artistic director of the Royal Theatre in Northampton offered me a small acting role in 'The Dresser', a drama set in a wartime Shakespearean acting company. I was delighted to be able to accept the challenge of acting in theatre, a world away from the circus. After the run of the play, members of the Royal Theatre Company, were going to put on a week of 'Old Time Music Hall', contributing various songs and comedy sketches. I worked on a comic plate spinning routine, disguised as a manic Spaniard with a bored lady assistant played with expertise by the lovely Kate Dunn.

It was a spoof of all such acts, and as my expertise at spinning plates was almost non-existent, I decided to use tin plates. I thought that a chimp might be a huge attraction and I approached Roger about the possibility of having Betsy with me for the week.

Despite a local newspaper review which called Betsy and I 'unentertaining and unnecessary' — obviously a reviewer without taste, Betsy and I had an enjoyable week together. Apart from sleeping hours Betsy and I spent the entire day together and found so much to keep us occupied in the theatre. Betsy endeared herself to the technical staff by proving to be a dab hand with a paintbrush and assisting with the design of the sets for a forthcoming attraction. She assisted in the wardrobe department, and was first in the queue when it came to tea-break in the Green Room.

Both of us wore old fashioned bathing suits for our contribution to the show, and we brought the whole performance to an end, with highlights from the old circus routine including the somersaults, tightwire routine and scooter tricks, "unentertaining" indeed!

Whilst we were performing our act, our distinguished chairman, actor Anthony Lindford would sit at his table on the side of the stage watching our act with enthusiasm. However, it was Betsy who was doing the watching as one evening she dashed across to Tony and grabbed his glass of port which accompanied him throughout his performance, and downed it in one!

Betsy would also watch very intently as I prepared myself for the show, something she had never witnessed before, as in our circus days she would be in her own quarters as I applied my make-up. In the theatre we were sharing a dressing room and so my making-up proved an endless source of fascination for her. On one particular evening I was called to the telephone as I was halfway through my preparation and I returned five minutes later to find Betsy applying make-up to herself. I let her continue and sat fascinated as she applied the make-up in the exact same order as I had done each night. First the foundation, then shading and last the eye-liner. I am not going to say who was the more accurate.

The final occasion I worked with the chimps as a group was the Welsh television Christmas Circus organised by Gandeys. The Big Top was erected in Wales in the July of 1982, which might seem a bit odd considering the show was for Christmas viewing, but such is the order of things for television. The show featured mainly Welsh artistes, including Gwyn Owen with his aerial act and Alun Davies with his dogs. Mary Chipperfield, who is not, I hasten to add Welsh, nevertheless provided animal acts to strengthen the show. Gandeys, particularly asked for the chimps and so we gave our farewell performance for the company with whom we had also made our debut in 1978. The chimps performed superbly, and looking at them on the television screening, I realised that they were now, with the exception of Anna, very large animals indeed.

One interesting factor about our final performance was that as the show was being aimed purely at a Welsh audience, no English was spoken. Our Ringmaster, a Welsh actor, making all the announcements in the beautiful language, and even I was forbidden to speak any English commands during the act as this would have been picked up on the microphones, so I was given some Welsh commands to use with a very bemused trio of chimps. They did not need any commands anyway as they could have done the act without me being there.

Shortly after the last time the chimps worked I realised I had to be firm with myself and 'let go' of them. It was time for them to start a new life, and I must not confuse them by interfering with their settling down process, so consequently I made fewer and fewer visits to see them.

When I was not around I doubt if they missed me, their lives were full and I do not expect that they sat around wondering 'where the old devil Hibling was'. On the other hand though, they never forgot me as was evident from their greeting whenever we met.

Anna was of course far from 'retiring' age, but such was her attachment to Fred and Betsy, in particular Betsy, that it was felt that she should be retired at the same time.

At the time of writing, the chimps have settled into two, separate, groups. Fred is still in the Chipperfield empire, having taken up a friendship with a rather truculent female chimp called Mary, who apparently had not inspired interest from any other suitor previously.

Betsy and Anna are now resident in a French zoo after a plea to Chipperfields for females to join a predominantly male group. Jimmy Chipperfield himself accompanied the animals to their new home.

I must admit, I was saddened to think the three had been split up, but I realised it was probably for the best. Fred regarded Betsy as a sister which cast doubts on whether or not they would form a breeding partnership. It is not uncommon in the wild for adolescent male chimps to leave a family group to find another in which to settle. Chipperfields have had spectacular successes with the breeding of chimps and other animals and it is important to reflect on the need for zoos, safari parks and even circuses to embark on breeding projects in order to preserve wild stocks.

Today there can be few animals brought into this country as a direct result of capture from the wild, and those that are will be subject to the strictest Government laws. Quite rightly too, as in the past the traffic in wild animals was alarming and none suffered more than the chimp.

Chimpanzees destined for European and American markets were caught as infants, with their mothers more than likely shot so as to obtain the unfortunate baby. Then they suffered appallingly in transport, often at the hands of unscrupulous dealers who sold to the highest bidder without a thought as to where the animals would be finally destined. Many young animals died of shock and those that survived caught diseases very easily as a result of unhygenic housing during transport.

Now, with the aid of international cooperation, laws and treaties the catching of wild animals is better controlled, and any illegal dealing is severely punished. That is not to say that illegal trade in skins, furs, ivory and live animals does not continue. It is also sad to reflect that many species survive only in captive or controlled environments.

Man encroaches wild habitat, changing jungle into farmland, forests into housing estates and the space for flora and fauna decreases. Therefore zoos, and to a lesser degree circuses, have a role in conservation and education. I firmly believe that only by seeing animals for real can ordinary folk really appreciate them. The size of an elephant, the power of a tiger, even the distinctive smell of individuals can only be appreciated in the flesh, not as images in a book, a TV programme or as a museum exhibit.

It is all very well for certain show business celebrities to criticise as unnecessary zoos and the like, as on their salaries a trip to what is left of Africa or India's wild places is not out of the question. Yet the average family who struggles to make ends meet can only thrill to the sight of an animal in a zoo or circus. I hope that in being entertained by the animals the public at large will not be impervious to the plight of wildlife in general, and I think the campaigns to save the tiger, whale and the like prove this.

It is very heartening to note that some animals owe their survival as a species thanks to zoos. The European bison, Arabian Oryx, and Hawaiian goose are three examples of animals thriving in places where they were once extinct thanks to zoo-bred animals being released in the wild.

In the last few years there have been examples of chimpanzees being returned to the wild. One of the more notable successes is that of Stella Brewer's project in Senegal, West Africa. Miss Brewer, the daughter of a Gambian forester, came into contact with several confiscated, illegally caught young chimps. With the help of the Senegalese Government, set up a camp in the Nickola Kobo National Park from where she hopes to re-release the animals. The London Zoo approached Miss Brewer with the offer of two young zoo-born chimps, Yula and Cameron who it was hoped could also be released into the reserve. It took many months of hard work and patient training to educate the animals to cope with a wild existence, with Stella having to introduce the animals to, amongst other things, the sort of wild food they would have to eat. On one occasion this meant that Miss Brewer had to eat termites to show Yula how tasty they were. A delightful book by Miss Brewer, 'The Forest Dwellers' was published in 1978, in which the story of her experiment is related.

Hopefully this is only the first of many such projects and it would be wonderful if future offspring from Fred, Betsy or Anna could be established in wild groups in Africa, that is providing there are enough places in Africa left for animals to roam free.

Back here at home, the transference of circus chimps to breeding groups is not difficult if handled patiently. It is a slow process, with both the newcomer, and the members of the existing group needing time to adjust with one another. Given space and time, the new chimp will find its place in the social order of the group. In the wild chimps live in large social families and even there, there are constant comings and goings.

With my chimps settled into a new environment I had time to reflect on my own new existence. I was still stubbornly thinking about acting. I had the good fortune to be included on the books of the London Theatrical agency Curtis and King, thanks to the influence of Jacquie Harbord, the Blackpool skater who was an old friend of Sally, one of the Curtis and King team. Through Curtis and King I auditioned for the New Shakespeare Company which, directed by David Conville, has its home in the open-air theatre in Regents Park, London.

The day of the audition was a shocker. Pouring rain, and an empty open-air theatre as I gave my audition piece to David Conville, I reflected, and was amused that I was leaving the Big Top and the

Sally Chipperfield with lion cub and jaguar cub. Just two of the many cubs bred by her family. *(David Jamieson)*

possibility of inclement weather, to exchange it for a theatre that was even more at the mercy of the elements. Whilst performing a play at the theatre rain sometimes causes a performance to be cancelled. The acting company battles on bravely in the rain until they are called off by the Stage Manager, as there is always the possibility that it is just a shower and will pass quickly.

In spite of, or perhaps because of, the rain my audition pleased David Conville and he offered me the job of Acting Stage Manager. This is a role which meant assisting the Stage Manager with various technical duties, and also small acting roles in the company's productions of Shakespeare's 'Midsummers Night Dream', the 'Taming of the Shrew' and also George Bernard Shaw's 'The Admirable Bashville'.

The summer season spent in the open-air theatre was very beneficial to me. I was able to watch and learn from such excellent actors and actresses as the like of Helen Ryan, James Cairncross and Kate O'Mara. I was able to find several friends in the company, most of whom were amused to have an ex-chimp trainer in their midst.

The highlight of each annual summer season at the Park is a gala Music Hall held to boost funds for the company. The season I was with the theatre the ubiquitous Chris Biggens produced the show which featured all of the company, plus many celebrities from the world of show business that generously gave their service for free. Amongst those that performed were Kenny Everett, Alvin Stardust, Peggy Mount, Dereck Guyler, Lisa Goddard, Joan Davies and Rula Lenska. I was able to revive the mad Spaniard and his plate spinning and was delighted to have Kate Dunn come up to the park and add her talents to the act's success.

True to fashion, the show had not finished when the heavens opened and the show had to be curtailed, with the audience showing true British determination, staying in their seats braving the weather long enough to enjoy a hastily brought forward finale — a medley of 'sunshine' songs.

The open-air theatre is one of London's greatest delights, attracting thousands of visitors from all over the world. Set in a wooded part of London's Regent Park it is very reminiscent of an ancient Greek amphitheatre.

It is an ideal home for the production of Shakespeare's 'Midsummers Night Dream' which the New Shakespeare Company religiously stages each year. Titania's and Oberon's speeches have never been more effective than when uttered in this leafy setting. One night, as I watched the play from the wings I was mesmerised when as Oberon commanded his fairies, two sparrows flitted across the arena, their unplanned entrance creating such a magical effect — no animal trainer could have achieved better timing. Later, as Oberon in his role of King of the Fairies summoned his legions to guard the Royal

Palace, thousands of little lights were switched on, the result was breathtakingly spectacular.

After the season 'in the Park' I was given a small acting role in HTV's adaptation of Daphne Du Maurier's 'Jamaica Inn'. I was to play Seth a young Cornish lad who spots the wreckers doing their dirty deeds and who rushes to warn the sleepy village nearby, collapsing in front of the heroine's (played by Jane Seymour), cottage.

I learned that a later episode of the series was to include a Christmas fair and I suggested to the producer Peter Graham Scott, that a gypsy with a dancing bear would add authenticity to the sequence. "Yes", he agreed "but where can I get a bear from?" I told him that as long as I could appear as the gypsy — I would find a bear. I instantly rang Roger Cawley and found out that Bobby from the panto days would be available. It must be mentioned that the entire Chipperfield empire is run from the little office at Longleat Safari Park, or to be more exact from a swivel chair in which Mr. Roger Cawley sits and directs proceedings. "Ring Roger" is a command frequently heard in circus circles all over the country.

The only problem was that it would be difficult for Seth to reappear as a bear trainer in the same series (although I suggested it would make an interesting sub-plot!) The Seth sequences were filmed on a misty October morning on the Cornish coast near Polzeath, and no expense was spared. The company actually wrecked an 85ft square-rigged ship. The fair sequences were shot a few weeks later in the National Trust village of Lacock, Wiltshire, and my identity problem was solved by growing a beard. Lacock is beautiful. There are no overhead cables or television aerials, and every house is ancient, none built since the 18th Century — no wonder it is a mecca for film studios.

This delightful setting had inspired the television production team to create a perfect early 19th Century Christmas Fair, complete with Punch and Judy, wrestling and mummer's booths, jugglers, fire-eaters, stalls selling a variety of wares, a horse market and of course Gypsy Hibling and his bear.

I learned later that there had been one or two doubts among the production staff as to whether or not a bear on the set was a good idea — "would he be behaved?" They did not know Bobby. The animal was as good as gold, patiently waiting until his turn came to be filmed, and 'dancing' to order when we required. The only animal 'trouble' came from the horses who were required to run from one end of the fair to the other — but when the time came and the horses released, they had their own ideas where they were to run to.

It was working with Bobby again that re-awoke the yearning for circus. I have said that the lure of the circus is strong and once you are smitten, it is hard to escape, perhaps John Ringling North says it all in

Gipsy Hibling with his bear. A scene from H.T.V's Jamaica Inn *(Author's collection)*

his book 'Circus Kings' when he writes,

"The Circus is a jealous wench, indeed that is an understatement, she is a ravenous hag who sucks your vitality as a vampire drinks blood, who kills the brightest stars in her crown, and allows no private life to those who serve her, wrecking their homes, ruining their bodies and destroying the happiness of their loved ones by her insatiable demands. She is all these things, yet I love her as I love nothing else on earth."

After 'Jamaica Inn', as I pondered my re-entry into circus I was out of work for several months, then gratefully accepted a job with a London-based Music Hall company, 'Song and Supper'. An enterprising small concern, created by the delightful Michelle Summers and Diedre Dee, who added their singing and dancing talents to a group of a dozen or so performers who offered traditional English entertainment to foreign visitors. I enjoyed myself immensely. I sang and danced, and yes, dusted off the old plate spinning props, this time having as my assistant the larger-than-life character of Mo, our choreographer. Mo had the unfortunate task of teaching me to dance, but despite this, was more than happy to bring her own style of humour to the plate spinning routine, full of energy and with an infectious giggle!

Whilst appearing with 'Song & Supper' I received a call from the Hippodrome in Great Yarmouth to see if I would be Ringmaster for the 1983 production of the Super Circus there.

Since the first Chipperfield shows in the building the Jays had gone from strength to strength, producing their own shows, rather than booking in a complete show like 'Circus World'. The 'Super Show' was the title adopted by the Jays for the series of summer circuses. In 1981, following Circus World, Yasmine Smart, granddaughter of the legendary Billy Smart, headlined the show. The Jays spent many thousands of pounds repairing the mechanisms that allow the ring to sink at Yarmouth and then be flooded to provide a water finale for the show. The ring sinks to a depth of six foot and in 1981 was the first time the water had been included since the fifites. It was a huge success.

In 1982 the show was built around the ample resources of the Roberts Brothers Circus including Bobby Roberts and his Royal Command Elephants. These six magnificent animals have twice appeared before the Queen, and are arguably the best elephant act in Europe.

I was honoured to be asked to officiate as Ringmaster, and thanks to the Jays I have since found another niche in the world of circus, as fulfilling as the role of chimp trainer. I am about to complete my fourth season as Ringmaster in the Hippodrome. As a result of my appearances there, I was approached to guest in the future as a Ringmaster with the mighty three-ring Royal Hanneford Circus in the U.S.A.

Back in 1983 though I was extremely nervous of the task before me. I was pleased to learn that Mary Chipperfield was headlining the show. It was in fact Mary who persuaded the Jays to use me as Ringmaster, and I think she was pleased to know that someone would be there to assist her with her tigers and horses. Mary helped me enormously in my first year, as did Joy Sloan, my old friend of Circus World days who had become General Manager of the Hippodrome. The inimitable Joy is the ideal General Manager, fiercely loyal, frighteningly efficient, and determined that the highest possible standards are always kept by staff and artistes alike. With her French-born husband Tony at her side, Joy is a Great Yarmouth institution much respected in the town. It is very important in a set-up like Yarmouth that the Ringmaster, responsible for the smooth running of backstage and of course the performance, has a good relationship with the General Manager. I have been able to combine a working relationship with Joy with a firm friendship and that is a great delight to me.

It is very much a 'team effort' that has given the Yarmouth shows so much success. Jack Jay, and his lovely wife Freida have more or less retired from active involvement from the running of the show, keeping a benevolent eye on son Peter and his wife, and co-director Christine.

Water fountain.
(Author's collection)

Peter has often said "I come up with the ideas and it is the team that makes them happen". The 'team' includes Joy, myself, Bryan Evans, in charge of the light and sound, a key ingredient in any Jay-produced circus, and Michael Fontaine who directs the show band. Michael, is, I would say, the finest circus musical director in Europe, very understanding of what makes a circus 'tick' and someone with a deep love of the business. His bands are sought after by circuses all over Europe and to date have appeared in France, Belgium, Holland, Sweden and regularly with the mighty Circus Krone in Germany.

The on going success of the Yarmouth shows has led Peter and Christine to directing the circus held each summer at the famed Blackpool Tower Circus. Success has repeated itself, so much so that the Blackpool show had to have its season extended in 1984, making it the longest runnning summer show in the country.

Being a Ringmaster in any circus is exacting work, but at the Hippodrome it is even more so. In a Peter Jay circus, the Ringmaster is not only performance director, company manager but also singer, dancer and comedian. Masterminding the smooth running of a show is very hard work, but I am lucky to have a loyal team of young men who help me as ring staff most of whom return each year, so I cannot be too much of a tyrant to work for. The ring staff are responsible for prop moving in the show, but the public are unaware perhaps that there are a thousand other tasks the 'boys' have to do during the day, ranging from sweeping the ring carpet, to exercising animals on the beach with the grooms. At Yarmouth, unlike her sister Blackpool which has a hydraulically controlled sinking ring, the ring is dropped and winched back up again by hand. Twice a day, six days a week and once on Sunday makes hard work for the staff.

The great pleasure of working at Yarmouth is that the team spirit extends through to the staff, and each summer the same staff seem to return. People like Ian, head Usher; Jane, head Usherette; Pam in the box office — all enjoy the unique atmosphere of the building. The building is kind to circus artistes too, making a good act look even better. The role call of acts that have appeared at the Hippodrome over the years reads like a who's who of circus. In my short time I have been honoured to work with some truly great circus artistes and to name just a few would be wrong, so I will simply tip my top hat in recognition to all the acts, all the circus dancers (and swimmers who have braved the water in the Yarmouth ring), all the musicians and all the staff who have made my association with the Hippodrome a happy one.

I doubted whether I would show animals again, but in 1985 I worked a Big and Little horse combination (involving Sam, a dependable old Shire horse and Johnny a cheeky Shetland, both belonging to Mary) in the Yarmouth show, together with an odd grouping of yak, Highland bull, buffalo, Ankole cow and Congo a

Author in the Hippodrome ring at Yarmouth. *(Courtesy Ivan Gould)*

Big and little act. Author with Shire horse and Shetland pony.
(Courtesy John Exton)

Author riding Jock the Highland bull.
(Courtesy John Exton)

King enjoying a ride on the author's back. (Simon Finlay)

King in a thoughtful mood. (Simon Finlay)

zebra. Also with me in 1985, much to my happiness was King a young chimp. King joined me as a result of his surrogate mother Mary Chipperfield going to Spain. She asked if I would care for him in her absence, giving him a summer holiday by the sea. We had a whale of a time together. He would have an early morning cuppa with either the night watchman or Alex Larenty who was showing an elephant act in the '85 show. Alex was always in the building early in the morning preparing to take his animals out onto the beach. King was adopted as one of the crew by the ring staff and demonstrated his prowess with a broom. In the show he became my 'assistant' helping, or rather hindering me, and at one point even took over the job of announcing the acts. To ensure he never got bored he was with me most of the day, and I was very happy to have him accompany me with my daily tasks. It was nice having a chimp 'around the house' again. He returned to Mary after her engagement in Spain was over and he is now at the Over Wallop Farm, fulfilling the role of assistant cook in the Chipperfield household!

Even now though, King is associating with other chimps to ensure that his eventual integration with a chimp colony will be an easy one. In his short career so far he has become something of a national celebrity, helping make "It's for Yoo-hoo" become a catch phrase after appearing in a television commercial.

I am certain that like Fred, Betsy and Anna before him his transference from one busy world, full of glitter and sawdust, to another with a group of chimps in a safari park or somewhere will not be difficult.

One of the things I admire about animals is their ability to accept in a dignified philosophical way their lot in life. If only we humans could do similar. I can remember a school poem in which I read of a man who 'wished he could turn and live with animals, they are so placid and self-contained'. I am lucky, I have turned and lived with animals, I count many of them as close friends and allies.

I dare to suggest that only in a circus-style environment in which animals achieve equal status as working partners with their human counterparts, can we really begin to value the contribution that animals give to our lives.

I certainly hope to be working with circus animals for many years to come.

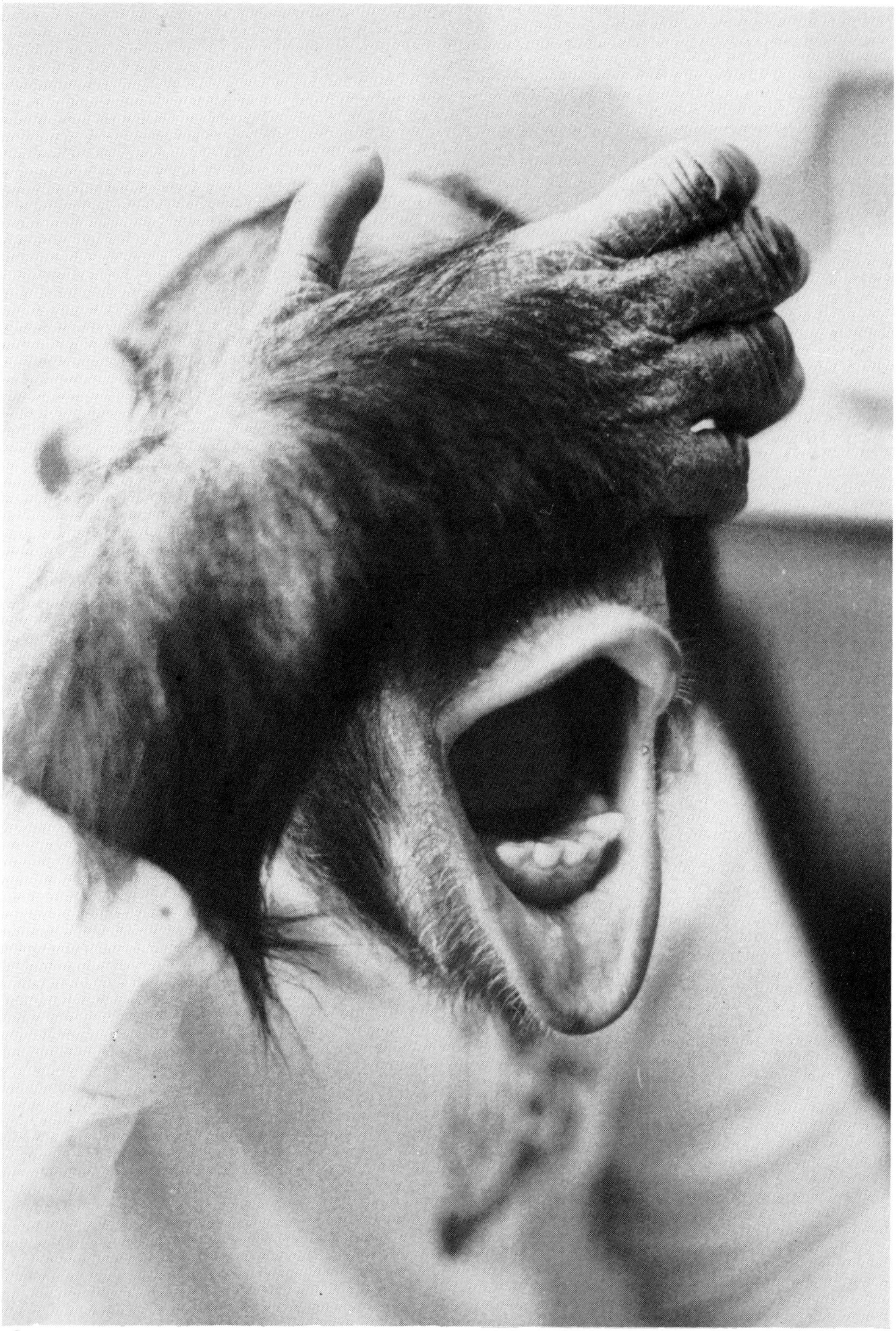

"Say goodnight Paul". *(Simon Finlay)*

Postscript

It is night-time at the circus. The show has finished and the audience makes its way home. The children, once excited with anticipation, are now sleepy, visions of dancing horses, elephants, acrobats and funny clowns fill their heads. Clutching balloons they climb wearily into parents' cars, perhaps taking a last look at the Big Top whose coloured lights are now flickering out one by one. It begins to rain.

From the caravans that nestle around the giant tent comes a variety of inviting smells as suppers representing the culinary delights of many lands are being cooked. Within these mobile homes, the sounds of television sets compete with chatting tongues speaking an assortment of languages as artistes change out of glittering costumes, remove make-up and snatch a couple of hours relaxation before sleep will refresh them, ready for another day of hard work tomorrow.

The animal grooms are bedding down their charges for the night. The lions, tigers and bears have all been fed and most are already asleep, bodies heaped lazily over one another. The shutters of their great wagons are lowered, excluding the chance that any of these precious beasts should get cold in the night.

Inside the stable tent Sahara the giraffe has also settled down for the night, chewing contentedly on hay, his long legs tucked underneath him. In the horse lines Ruth is fastening the horse blankets onto the Arabs, scolding Bagdad for attempting to steal hay from his neighbour Sceptre's hay-net, despite having an ample supply of the sweet-smelling grass of his own. Bagdad delights in being mischievous.

Nearby, Mary Chipperfield is supervising the bedding down of her great grey elephants. A blue and white dressing gown thrown over her finale costume, and a headscarf tied severely over her blonde hair, she still has full show make-up on. Only when she is certain all the animals are settled for the night, will she herself retire to her mobile home. The elephants are almost buried beneath a mountain of straw and hay, and Mary jokes with her elephant groom how lucky to be an elephant and be able to eat your bed should you awake in the night and feel peckish. When all is quiet and still in the stables the elephants themselves will lie down and sleep, usually leaving one of the herd awake to watch over the rest as they doze.

The chimps are having their warm milk, and I distribute a few digestive biscuits, just in case they too should feel hungry during the night hours. Joey the baboon, 'joe-soap' as Margaret Chipperfield has nicknamed him, also shares the milk and biscuits, before, like the chimps he will rearrange his straw bedding into a warm, deep nest in which he will sleep until the morning.

Fred gives me a weary 'Goodnight' kiss and in no time he is asleep and dreaming. That chimp could set a world record for falling asleep so quickly! I collect up the mugs and make my way out of the stables. One of the circus generators is switched off and the tent is plunged into darkness, save for a solitary working light left on so that whoever is on 'stablewatch' for the night will see what he or she is doing.

I pause for a few seconds and wait. I am not disappointed. A low soft hooting can be heard from beneath a pile of warm straw.

"Goodnight Betsy."

The Ringmaster and circus artistes. *Yarmouth Mercury*